VOICE

VOICE

ADAM POTTLE
ON WRITING WITH DEAFNESS

 University of Regina Press

Printed and bound in Canada at Friesens. The text of this book is printed on 100% post-consumer recycled paper with earth-friendly vegetable-based inks.

Cover and text design: Duncan Campbell, University of Regina Press
Copy editor: Dallas Harrison
Proofreader: Donna Grant
Cover art: Digitally manipulated by Duncan Noel Campbell from a photo by viki-melkiu / iStockphoto.

Library and Archives Canada Cataloguing in Publication

Pottle, Adam, author
    Voice : Adam Pottle on writing with deafness.

(Writers on writing)
Includes bibliographical references and index.
Issued in print and electronic formats.
ISBN 978-0-88977-593-0 (softcover).—ISBN 978-0-88977-594-7 (PDF).—ISBN 978-0-88977-595-4 (HTML)

1. Pottle, Adam. 2. Deaf authors—Canada—Biography. 3. Deafness—Psychological aspects. 4. Authorship—Psychological aspects. 5. Creation (Literary, artistic, etc.). 6. Autobiographies. I. Title. II. Title: Adam Pottle on writing with deafness. III. Series: Writers on writing (Regina, Sask.)

PS8631.O7746Z46 2019   C813'.6   C2018-906030-1

10 9 8 7 6 5 4 3 2 1

University of Regina Press, University of Regina
Regina, Saskatchewan, Canada, S4S 0A2
TEL: (306) 585-4758 FAX: (306) 585-4699
U OF R PRESS   WEB: www.uofrpress.ca

We acknowledge the support of the Canada Council for the Arts for our publishing program. We acknowledge the financial support of the Government of Canada. / Nous reconnaissons l'appui financier du gouvernement du Canada. This publication was made possible with support from Creative Saskatchewan's Book Publishing Production Grant Program.

Debbie. Always.

WRITERS ON WRITING

The Writers on Writing series offers readers witty, conversational reflections on a wide range of craft-related topics, as well as practical advice for writers and the writing life at any level. The books are accessible and handy, yet they don't shy away from the challenges of writing. They'll become your friends. Think of sitting down in a coffee shop in conversation with a smart, friendly, veteran author. Part inspiration, part advice, part anecdote—total oxygen after all those stuffy writing textbooks.

Jeanette Lynes, Series Editor

FOR MORE INFORMATION ON THE
Writers on Writing SERIES, CONTACT:

University of Regina Press
3737 Wascana Parkway
Regina, SK S4S 0A2
uofrpress@uregina.ca
www.uofrpress.ca

PREVIOUS BOOKS IN THE
Writers on Writing BOOK SERIES:

Sleuth: Gail Bowen on Writing Mysteries,
by Gail Bowen (2018)

CONTENTS

WHAT KIND OF
DEAF MAN?

April 2017. I sit in a soundproof booth at the Ex-Cell Hearing Centre in Saskatoon. I settle into my chair and adjust my headset. I feel as though I'm in a flight simulator, about to pilot an imagined craft toward a war zone. "Squadron Commander Pottle here, awaiting the countdown to takeoff."

I hold a clicker in my right hand. Everything smells of plastic and rubber and something else—the bitter musk of having unwelcome news confirmed. The hearing aid technician sits just outside the booth and turns on the microphone.

"Okay, Adam, I'm going to play a series of sounds for you. Just push the button whenever you hear a noise."

I nod. I've been through this test more than a dozen times. As always, the technician starts with lower-pitched noises, then dials up the pitch. The sounds haven't changed:

WOOWOOWOOWOO ... woowoowoowoo ... woowoowoowoo ...

SSSTSSSTSSSTSSST ... sssTsssTsssTsssT ...

YIIYIIYIIYIIYII ...

"Okay, now I'm going to read a list of words and cover my mouth, and I want you to repeat them back to me as best as you can."

This is the part of the test I loathe the most. It's too close to what I deal with every day. I hate that she covers her mouth. It's like she's screwing with me, torturing me to see how much miscommunication I can stand. I stare at the floor the whole time.

"Say the word *dog leash.*"

"Dog least—leash."

Dammit, I think. *Even when I hear the fricking thing, I don't trust myself to—*

"Say the word *Sunday.*"

"Sunday."

Okay, good. Got that one.

"Say the word *remrarn.*"

"Remrarn."

Gah.

"Say the word *blundsadt.*"

"Blundsadt."

Come on.

"Say the word *facestall.*"

"Facestall."

Fuck.

"Say the word *mirnelpet.*"

All right, you've already made your point, you auditory asshole. Let's just move on to the goddamn diagnosis.

The technician stands and opens the door. "Thank you, Adam." She lifts the headset from my ears and hangs it on the wall. "If you'd like to follow me."

She leads me back into her office and asks me to sit at the table across from her. On the table are brochures for hearing aid brands featuring smiling people of all ages living excellent lives thanks to their improved hearing. I wonder about the exact date I stopped wearing hearing aids. It would've been just before I started university—fifteen years earlier. I think about where my hearing aids went and whether they were taken apart and rebuilt and whether I left them full of wax and, if I did, whether the wax balled together and came alive and started terrorizing children in its gleefully malevolent quest to live inside their heads forever.

"So, Adam," the technician says, "here's the audiogram I was able to put together."

She shows me the graph. Instead of two jagged lines running parallel to each other, as they had in my childhood, one line, indicating my left ear, maintains more or less the same shape it has for the past twenty-seven years. The other line, indicating my right ear, drops off much earlier. Both lines sink down into the PROFOUND area of the graph.

The technician pushes her glasses further up the bridge of her nose. "I imagine this isn't news to you," she says.

It isn't. In my late twenties, my hearing in my right ear began to diminish. Since I was a child, my right ear had always been my best ear, and when my hearing diminished it was as though my ear canal had been filled with tar. My head felt lopsided, like a bucket with all the muck heaped on one side.

In 2013 I went to a doctor, who sent me to have a CT scan. The scan revealed something called a superior canal dehiscence, a missing bone in my right inner ear. Symptoms include diminished hearing (to a deaf man, that's a larf—like robbing someone who just had his wallet stolen), high-pitched ringing (which I've had since my late teens), balance issues (which I haven't), and foggy thinking (don't all writers have that?).

"Not news," I say, "but difficult to hear all the same."

The technician purses her lips.

"I was told before that hearing aids won't help me," I say. "Is that true?"

"Yes," the technician says. "I mean, you can try wearing one in your left ear, and it'll increase the volume, but the clarity won't be any better, so really it won't do you much good."

"What sort of options are there if I do wanna try one?"

The technician gives me a list, along with a set of brochures. "Well, if you're going to be—you said you're a teacher, right?"

"University instructor."

"You may want to look at other kinds of teaching solutions," she says. "Like Sign Language interpretation."

"I'm not fluent in ASL. Besides, no university will pay for an entire term's worth of interpretation services."

She purses her lips again and hangs her head. It's both cute and annoying that she seems to bear some responsibility for the difficulties caused by my deafness.

"But maybe they can do something else for me—rig up a captioning application or something, now that I have the medical documentation."

She sits up straight. "Sure! Something'll get worked out."

"We'll see. Thank you."

I shake her hand and leave.

During the previous school year, I'd had more difficulty than usual understanding my students. I taught four courses during the year, and every single class I had to ask my students to repeat what they were saying—often three or four times. In one instance late in the fall term, a student got so exasperated she rolled her eyes to the ceiling and mouthed "Oh my god." I don't blame her. I felt her frustration and the frustration of her classmates. I hadn't taken the initiative to ensure my classes would run smoothly. I was a sessional lecturer and didn't think I had the right to ask for help—not if I wanted to be employed again. What school would spend money on accessibility supports for a sessional lecturer?

The more pressing question was what kind of support did I want?

Answering the question depended on what kind of deaf man I wanted to be: one who engages mainly through orally spoken language and tries to conform to hearing normalcy, or one who engages primarily through visual language—chiefly text and captioning.

• • •

In June, two months after my appointment at the Ex-Cell Hearing Centre, I sit in the waiting room of Saskatoon's best otolaryngologist. He's been booked solid for months, and his waiting room indicates it. Besides me, seven groups of people wait to see him. Two are families with young boys who, as evidenced by their laughter and their complete disregard for their parents' instructions (a disregard I know all too well), are clearly deaf. As I watch them, it's clear they possess the same bivouac that shelters me. The other five are older couples. The young and the old: the two most common groups affected by deafness.

"Mm-mm?"

I look up. A voice appears to call me, but no one's looking at me. Then the otolaryngologist, a tall man who looks to be in his mid- to late thirties, steps around the corner.

"Adam?"

I stand and follow him down the hall.

"How are you?" he says, shaking my hand.

"Oh, you know. Wondering."

"Come on in."

He invites me into his office, which has a number of strange contraptions in it. One looks like an old stainless steel oven that's been reappropriated for burning into people's ear cavities. Another looks like a dentist's x-ray camera.

"What exactly did you want to talk about today, Adam?"

"Just—I guess options. I've been having more difficulty with my hearing in the classroom, and I'm checking to see if there's anything I can do. You know, just exploring everything."

"Mm-hmm. I received your audiogram," he says, holding up the paper.

"Yeah. The technician says that hearing aids aren't an option."

"Well, actually they are an option, at least for your left ear. For your right, as you know, you have the dehiscence, so the best option there might be a cochlear implant."

I jar my teeth against each other. I'm wearing a black Slipknot hoodie with a Slipknot concert t-shirt underneath. Joey Jordison's drumbeats splatter and gurgle in my head, like a dragon digesting Pop Rocks.

"Okay," I say.

"So you can have the aid for the left ear and the implant on the right. Implants take many months, and we'd have to find out if you qualify, but I'm quite sure you do."

"Aren't implants expensive?"

"Implants are one hundred percent covered."

"And aids?"

"Hearing aids unfortunately aren't."

"That's fucked."

He nods and raises his eyebrows. "If you'd like, we can give you some information and a bit of paperwork to fill out—about five pages or so—just to see if you qualify. As I said, it'll take months to find out, but you want to get that process started soon if you do want it. And if you don't qualify, then that's that, and if you do then you can make your decision."

"Okay." I think for a moment. "Can a superior canal dehiscence cause brain damage?"

"If a certain part of the brain is used to receiving signals, then stops receiving them, then it can degenerate, like a muscle."

"Lovely."

Before I leave, he sticks a camera up my nose. I feel it creeping behind my eye, pressing against my tear duct. He withdraws it and gives me a Kleenex.

"Anything else?" I say.

"I think we're done. We'll just step down the hall here and get the implant forms. You can fill them out and send them to us as soon as possible. If you have any questions, you can email me."

I thank him, collect the paperwork, and walk home.

It's raining. I don't put my hood up.

• • •

In 2016, in an interview for my play *Ultrasound*, I said that deafness is like a country. It doesn't have borders or land, but it has its own habits, customs, language, its own way of telling stories. With my diminishing hearing, I feel like I'm becoming more of a deaf native as time goes on.

Before my appointment with the otolaryngologist, I'd accepted that I'd continue to lose my hearing. Part of me welcomed it. My wife, Debbie, and I had taken an ASL (or American Sign Language) class together, and I figured that I would keep working on my Sign Language and become more involved in the Deaf community—that is, with people who are culturally Deaf and fluently use Sign Language, as opposed to people who just have hearing loss. I figured I'd quit teaching and focus on writing full time, isolating myself within the greenhouse of my imagination and cultivating an entire world of characters and stories. Although I might misunderstand my students, I never have to worry about misunderstanding my characters. I figured that by age forty-five—fifty at the most—I'd be completely Deaf.

Within the past few years, Deaf culture has become more prominent, thanks to figures such as Marlee Matlin, Nyle DiMarco, Katie Leclerc, and Millicent Simmonds. The television show *Switched at Birth* has shown the potential of telling stories about Deaf and disabled people. Deaf people are performing on stages across the world (*Spring Awakening, Children of a Lesser God*) and winning popular talent contests (*America's Next Top Model, Dancing with the Stars*). In America writers such as John Lee Clark and Ilya Kaminsky have garnered considerable attention, and here in Canada Deaf artists such as Landon Krentz, Catherine MacKinnon, Chris Dodd, Elizabeth Morris, Jack Volpe, Dawn Jani Birley, Sage Lovell, and Joanne Weber have snagged the attention of theatre audiences across the country. No longer satisfied with token gestures, the Deaf are making their cultural presence known.

I now sit at the dining room table, reading over the implant paperwork. Part of the package includes a booklet from a manufacturer extolling the benefits of implants: "Our cochlear implants provide the fullest, richest range of sounds, support better music and speech perception, and help protect your remaining natural hearing." Behind-the-ear audio processors come in numerous colours: Pacific blue, Bordeaux red, green, orange, baby pink, baby blue, and creme. One of the audio processors is called SONNET.

I flip through the implant forms. They strike me as citizenship forms. By filling them out and signing them and sending them off, I feel like I'm defecting or relinquishing my provisional membership in the rising Deaf nation and reclaiming or reaffirming my privileged hearing status. The Deaf community views cochlear implants with suspicion if not scorn. Implants are the Confederate flags of hearing privilege, a symbol of an individual's desire to conform to the hearing world rather than embrace the beauty of Deafness. Videos of children having their cochlear implants activated and hearing their parents' voices for the first time often outrage Deaf people, who see these videos as negations of their right to exist and express themselves how they wish.

I rub my neck, which has accumulated massive knots from having to twist and turn to see people's mouths. I think about what Ryan Knighton said about blindness and writing: "I don't separate being a writer and being a blind guy. To me, they are inextricably tied together. If you gave me my sight back, I don't know if I would be a writer anymore." I worry that a cochlear implant will shatter the greenhouse my deafness has created around my imagination. I worry that, after living without hearing aids and FM systems for more than a decade, using hearing devices will be too overwhelming. I imagine that getting an implant would be the auditory equivalent of having pepper, lavender, paint thinner, and alligator shit jammed up my nostrils. At first. I did get used to my hearing aids, but I was six years old then.

I stare at the forms. It's cloudy outside; the dimness softens the pages. A sharp ringing slices through my right ear, and I cover it out of instinct, even though I know the sound's coming from within my ear canal. The forms' font is rigid, authoritative, even petty. If it were a person, it would be a tax man who constantly fantasizes about stapling his co-workers' shoelaces to the floor.

I think about the book I'm working on, the one in which I explore the relationship between my deafness and my writing. Although it's entirely possible that having a cochlear implant will open up new dimensions in my imagination, it could also disrupt the chemistry of my brain that drives my writing, the chemistry that's taken me years of difficult, revelatory work to develop. The book explores childhood experiences, obscure memories, and the origins of my published stories, but it doesn't pull me closer to an answer. Not yet anyway.

I push the forms away. I don't know if it's worth it or if anything will change. Maybe I should be satisfied with not having an answer and continue living in the barbed, constrictive space straddling the hearing and Deaf worlds. It's gotten me this far.

I used to tell myself that I needed perpetual discomfort to create, that reacting against a world not built for me or for other disabled people has spurred my imagination. But imagination is transferable. It exists just as much in a state of hope as it does in a state of despair. If I can make the world easier to navigate, through whatever means possible, isn't that a good thing?

PART 1

BECOMING DEAF

H ow did you deal with it, Lemmy?
> *Eh? Deal with what?*

Telling your story. Like your life story.

Well, I use music, man. I wanna say something, that's everything, you know. Just pick up my guitar and off I go, whatever comes out. You understand me okay?

Yeah, fine.

'Cause I know you're deaf and all, and I talk like I got fucking rubber teeth.

No worries.

Hey. How you tell a deaf guy he's stepping on your toe? HEY, DEAF GUY, GET THE FUCK OFF MY TOE.

That's the rub, though. I prefer to write stuff I make up, not shit that actually happened to me. The stuff I make up's truer and more entertaining.

Why you writing about yourself at all? Isn't it supposed to be a writing textbook or some shit?

I'm supposed to talk about how my deafness has impacted me as a writer. Can't talk about that without a bit of background.

Will you talk about music at all?

Sure. I'm a drummer.

Great.

But I'm not a rock star like you. My life's pretty dull.

Well, you signed the deal, didn't you? You sign the deal, you do the fucking work. You don't just take their money. And if you do the work, you do it well.

I don't have a problem with the work. I'm just not used to talking about myself. It's . . . bleh.

Just do it your way, man. Make it yours. It's your life. Be grateful that someone's interested, you know. At least there's not a camera showing what's in your fucking garbage can, peeking into your shit. Nothing's sacred. Your life, my life. Life's too short for shit to be sacred.

• • •

"Say the word *murfday.*"

"First day."

"Say the word *bessball.*"

"Baseball."

I sit in a small soundproof booth. It looks like a recording booth, except I'm here to receive sound rather than emit it. Wires and old headsets hang from hooks. A plate-glass window looks onto another room; the audiologist, a uniformly kind woman, sits in that room in front of what looks like a mixing board, pushing buttons and adjusting frequencies like a sound engineer. Behind the audiologist, my parents sit against the wall, watching. I'm six years old.

"Say the word *ranmah.*"

"Ranmah."

"Say the word *muh-er*."

"Muh-tter."

I stare at the floor and blush. The audiologist makes notes, then comes into the booth and gives me the clicker and asks me to push the button whenever I hear a noise. She plays a series of beeps, rustles, and drones, starting in one ear, then moving to the other, softening the volume with each sound:

WOOWOOWOOWOO ... WOOWOOWOOWOO ... WOOWOOWOOWOO ... WOOWOOWOOWOO ...

SSSTSSSTSSSTSSST ... SSSTSSSTSSSTSSST ... SSSTSSSTSSSTSSST ... SSSTSSSTSSSTSSST ...

YIIYIIYIIYIIYII ... YIIYIIYIIYII ... YIIYIIYIIYII ...

I push the clicker whenever I hear, or whenever I think I hear, a noise. I try to time the beeps and rustles and drones so I can be right, so I can ease my parents' anxiety, so I can quell my own discomfort.

Embedded in the wall of the booth and sitting in a box of black glass is a plush monkey holding a pair of cymbals. If I say the right word or push the clicker at the right time, the audiologist flicks a switch, and the monkey lights up and nods its head and crashes its cymbals. Shrouded by its black box, it looks like a horror movie character—Chucky's simian partner. It looks like it might throw the cymbals down and punch through the glass and reach out for me.

Ten minutes later I sit in the audiologist's office. Hearing aid batteries, plastic containers, small screwdrivers, and other unique equipment line the shelves. A window looks out onto the small city of Terrace, British Columbia; our home in Kitimat is forty-five minutes away. On the wall is a poster detailing the intricate anatomy of the inner ear. With its blue, pink, and green colouring, it looks like the gastrointestinal system of a tubular alien.

In her office, the audiologist explains my audiogram to my parents and me. On a lined graph, she's drawn an image illustrating the range of my hearing: two jagged lines run parallel to each other, one for the left ear and one for the right. The lines start from the left side of the graph and skid to the right, forming the shape of a cliff. On the left side of the audiogram is a small, relatively flat plain—the meadow before the rocky plunge. This little plain is just above the cutoff line, meaning that in the lower, deep-bass pitches I have close to normal hearing. But as the pitches become higher, my ability to hear drops; as the graph moves to the right, the line sinks . . . and sinks . . . and sinks. The image looks like the Cliffs of Moher in Ireland. You can almost see the ocean waves skirting up the rocky shore. You can imagine someone slipping off the edge and falling for what seems like forever before crashing onto the rigid, toothy boulders below.

• • •

I was born with what's called sensorineural hearing loss in both ears, meaning I lack certain nerves that pick up sound and transfer it to my brain. I'm a genetic anomaly: no one else on either side of my family was born deaf. My parents' chemistry mixed just right—or wrong, depending on your viewpoint.

Although I was born deaf, it took a while to confirm it. I was about three when my mom began to suspect. It was difficult to tell, though. According to her, I did everything early—talked at six months, walked at eight months, and knew my ABCs at eighteen months—and

I was adept at reading lips and body language, which compensated for whatever deficiencies she and my family might have found. When I was three, my mom tested me by whispering in my ear. She'd come up behind me and say things like "Adam, who you gonna call?" At first I answered her—"Ghostbusters!"—but over the next few years my deafness became more apparent.

I can hear most people speak, but I can only understand them when I read their lips; otherwise, it sounds like mumbling. One spring day during my kindergarten year, when my family was living in Ashcroft, BC, my class went into the gymnasium and sat in a circle in the centre. We played a game called Pass It On, in which one kid would whisper a message to the kid sitting to her right, and that kid would whisper the message to the next kid, and so on until the message made it all the way back to the first kid; the idea was to keep the words consistent. When my turn came, all I heard was windy gibberish. I then had to turn to the girl to my right and whisper in her ear. I said, "Alligators eat Twinkies," approximating the number of windy syllables I'd heard.

The girl made a face, then whispered the same message to the boy on her right. When the message reached the end of the circle, the girl who started it stood up and said, "No! That's not it! Who didn't say it! Who said the wrong thing!" I kept my eyes to the floor. The girl was known for kicking other kids, and she was wearing shiny black shoes that looked like they'd hurt.

Such misunderstandings have become part of my life, and sometimes they have distressing consequences. In the fall of 1990, my Grade One class participated in the Cormorant Elementary School bike rodeo. I piloted my bike between pylons and along a straight line marked with chalk; I learned that cyclists had to ride on the right side of the road and that they must use arm signals. The signals came easily to me: I got all of them correct and was given reflective stickers to put on my helmet.

On a Tuesday morning about two weeks after the rodeo, I was sitting at the table eating cereal when my mom came up to me.

"Adam," she said, "I have an appointment this afternoon, so don't ride home. Auntie Jeannie will be picking you up. Watch for her after school. Okay?"

"Okay, Mom."

Mom had an appointment every Tuesday—nothing unusual. I finished my cereal, picked up my backpack, put on my helmet, and rode my bike to school.

When school ended, I went outside and unlocked my bike—combination 3-2-6—and looked around for my Auntie Jeannie. I couldn't find her or her car. I waited. The parents of other kids came and collected them. I didn't see Auntie Jeannie's car coming up the road. I grew indignant. I waited for a few more minutes, then strapped on my helmet and got on my bike and rode to her house.

In Kitimat two roads take you just about everywhere you need to go: Haisla Boulevard and Lahakas Boulevard. Cormorant Elementary School sat at the top of Lahakas, a steep curving road that rolls all the way to downtown Kitimat, where it meets Haisla. To get to Auntie Jeannie and Uncle Dan's house, I had to ride my bike all the way down the thin gravel shoulder of Lahakas, then turn right onto Haisla, then left onto Kuldo Boulevard and left onto Lillooet Street. The journey was a little over a mile.

I left the school grounds and crossed to the right side of Lahakas. It was grey and rainy—a typical Kitimat day. I must have looked strange, though, a six-year-old kid with a neon green-and-blue helmet riding a black bike that said "Vampire" in scratchy green letters on the handlebar. I didn't care. Auntie Jeannie had forgotten me, and I was going to make it to her house and let her know. The traffic was heavy for Kitimat, but I used the hand signals I'd learned two weeks before to indicate where I was going, and the cars on the road gave me a fair bit of room, probably because the drivers were terrified of hitting a young kid.

When I arrived at Auntie Jeannie's house, I marched up the front steps and knocked on the door. As soon as Auntie Jeannie opened it, I said, "You didn't pick me up!"

She peered past me. "Adam, what are you doing here? Where's your mom?"

"She had an appointment. You were supposed to pick me up!"

"No—what? How did you get here?"

"I rode my bike!"

She stared at me. "You rode all the way down here from school?"

"Yes! Why did you forget me?"

Auntie Jeannie sighed, then brought me into the house. I sat down on the couch. "Stay here for a minute," she said. She went into the kitchen and dialed the phone.

"Barb? You okay? It's okay, it's all right. Adam's here, Adam's here. He's fine. He rode his bike. He thought that I was supposed to pick him up."

What my mom had actually said that morning was "Adam, I don't have an appointment today, so I want you to come home. Auntie Jeannie's not picking you up. I'll be here watching for you, okay?" After waiting for me to show up, Mom had gone to the school, but she hadn't found me there. She'd asked my teacher and the office staff, but no one knew where I was. She'd quickly become distraught. At that time, kidnapping was the Great Fear in BC. Our teachers and principals always told us never to talk to strangers or get into strange vehicles, and there were posters in every school encouraging kids to walk in groups. Pictures of missing children often adorned bulletin boards and gas station doorways; the Michael Dunahee case was still several months away, but all across the province the spectre of kidnapping pervaded parents' minds.

Immediately after Auntie Jeannie called her, Mom drove down, and when she came in her eyes were red. She seized me and held me close. "Mom, why are you crying? Let me go. Mom?" Her grip crushed the air out of me—I snatched breaths over her shoulder. "Mom!" She sobbed. It was like she wanted to absorb me back into her body so she'd never have to worry about me again.

• • •

Shortly after the audiologist confirmed my deafness, I was fitted for hearing aids. The audiologist filled my ear with a special plastic to create the moulds; it felt like my ears were filling up with gum. The moulds were then processed and fitted to the aids.

When we went to pick them up, we sat in the audiologist's office, a place I'd quickly gotten used to. The audiologist showed me how to turn the aids on, which setting to use for talking on the phone, and how to adjust the volume. She turned them on without the moulds; my mom winced. The aids emitted a harsh squealing noise when they were switched on outside my ears, a noise that, much to my delight, since I couldn't hear it, would annoy my family for years to come. My dad would hear a squealing noise in the house and search all over, checking the phone, the fridge, the heating ducts, the television, and the Mixmaster before calling my mom.

"Barb! Did you hear that squealing noise this morning?"

"What?"

"Here. Listen."

"I don't . . . oh, did you check Adam's hearing aids?"

"Oh, for Christ's sake."

The audiologist fitted the aids into my ears and asked me to turn them on. I inhaled, then pushed the tiny switch to the right. A burst of clatter and static shunted through my head. I gasped.

"Is that okay, Adam?" the audiologist said. "Can you hear me?"

"It's so loud!"

The audiologist put her pen down on the table. It made an unbelievably resonant clang. I glanced around. Sounds seemed to come from everywhere. I heard wind, even though there was no breeze. My mom moved her purse to the floor, and I could hear every single item inside—change, keys, wallet, gum, lipstick, compact, pads—jostling and colliding.

"Is it always like this?" I said.

"Can you turn the volume down, Adam?" Mom said.

I stared at her. "Is everything always this noisy?"

I lowered the volume—all the way down. Mom thanked the audiologist, and we left the clinic. I walked gingerly, like a hermit emerging after years of being inside, adjusting the volume and watching the world with suspicion, as though sounds would snatch out from the walls and clap me on my ears.

When we arrived at home, I took out the hearing aids and put them on my dresser. Every sound, no matter how minuscule, was too loud, too clear. The soft rustle of the curtains sounded like a goblin sliding its claw down my ear canal; the door slammed rather than closed; clattering dishes made ominous music—I waited for the glasses to break and the plates to snap. I was hearing microscopically: the world had zoomed in several feet closer to my ears, and I hated it. I needed the distance.

• • •

When I was eight years old, Mom and I took a course in Signed English. We attended on Wednesday evenings, taking our Duo-Tangs full of illustrations and definitions and driving down to the Northwest Community College and filling out worksheets and practising signs. Mom had enrolled us for practical reasons—"It couldn't hurt," she said—and maybe she thought I'd find a sense of community, so I wouldn't feel alone.

Each evening we'd practise our ABCS and yes and no and Mom and Dad. My dad quickly picked up a few signs and employed them with visible glee.

"Dad," I'd say, "can I please have a creamsicle?"

"No," he'd sign, then add, "you pig."

"You rat," I'd sign.

I passed the course but soon forgot almost everything I learned. In Kitimat, where my family lived from 1989 to 1994, I never met any other kids who were deaf or hard of hearing. That didn't matter, though. I'd already found my community.

In Kitimat hockey is the first, second, and third favourite sport. Every game or practice was a family affair: my dad and Uncle Dan coached my brother Taylor, my cousin Ryan, and me through our novice years. Mom and Auntie Jeannie would always come to games, as did the Bakers, the McCormicks, the Medeiroses, the Scotts, the Yateses, the Zuidemas, the Vocionis, the Sparkeses, the Tormenes, and the Rodriguezes. The teams were named after local organizations—Knights of Columbus, CPU Local 298, CASAW, Eurocan, Alcan, Farwest—and though our rivalries could get heated they remained good-natured.

When *The Mighty Ducks* came to the Nechako Theatre, the Kitimat Minor Hockey League booked the theatre and invited every player in town to see it. Fishing trips, hockey sticks, jerseys, and Road Warrior goalie equipment were raffled off, and the film itself became a constant source of quotations among us players. Goalies yelled out "I am Goldberg the goalie!" Teams would imitate the "quack, quack, quack" chant on the bench before games. Taylor and I argued over who would be Adam Banks and who would be Fulton Reed.

Once I got my legs under me, I found I had a certain advantage on the ice. Not only was I tall for my age, but also I could read other players' body language and anticipate plays. I could find pockets of space within the offensive zone and exploit them either to score or to set up a teammate. If I was playing defence, I could see which areas of the ice were most dangerous and close them off. The spatial aspects of the game came easily to me. I always felt at home on the ice and made fast friends with my teammates.

In 1992, the same year *The Mighty Ducks* came out, my parents approached the local Elks organization for funding to send me to hockey school in Ottawa. It wasn't a regular hockey school, though. Although there were the typical daily on-ice sessions and dryland activities, this school, created by Jim Kyte, was different.

Kyte was a hockey player who at that time had played for the Winnipeg Jets, Pittsburgh Penguins, and Calgary

Flames. He was an enforcer; there are YouTube videos of him trading haymakers with Marty McSorley and Tim Hunter and numerous other heavyweights. He was also deaf and created a school specifically for young hockey players who were also deaf or hard of hearing: the Jim Kyte Hockey School for the Hearing Impaired.

The school was great. I got to meet NHLers such as Garry Galley, Glen Wesley, Gord Murphy, and Doug Gilmour; I still have my autographed Gilmour card from that school. We were on the ice every day, and every night we stayed in the dorms of the RCMP college. I met many kids my own age who, like me, wore hearing aids, and I enjoyed horsing around with them (creating chants or coming up with obscene gestures to flick at opposing players), but after the school ended and I went back to Kitimat I never kept in touch with any of them. I was unable or unwilling to connect to my fellow players. The one instance when I came close to establishing a friendship was the first night, when my roommate Tommy and I tossed an object—I think it was a hat—back and forth over the partition separating our dorm beds. With our hearing aids in their containers for the night, and the dark room making it impossible to read each others' lips, tossing the hat was our way of communicating. I was also uncomfortable when our group leader, Ella, spoke. Her voice had an unusual thickness that I later realized was a deaf accent. She pronounced pizza the way we pronounce Pisa. My own voice sometimes has the same thickness.

When I want something, I focus on that one thing and ignore everything else, even if other necessary or awesome things arise. If my wife and I need milk, I go and get milk and ignore the specials on apples and flour. If I want to see the *Mona Lisa* at the Louvre, I seek out the *Mona Lisa* and ignore the Rembrandts and Raphaels. When I went to Ottawa, I went there for the hockey and ignored the friendships. My deafness helps me to focus, which has allowed me to achieve many things, but sometimes my focus is much too narrow.

• • •

This shit's fucking me up.

You bring my weed?

I'm having a hard time remembering shit. It's like scraping the last bit of ketchup from the bottom of the fry box. I wish I had a documentary crew to put my life story together. Save me a shitload of work.

You want a group of jackoffs you never met before poking around, calling your ex-girlfriends, calling your mum and dad, having all these other people tell your story? Not the right approach, man. Even when you're the centre it's not all about you, you know. You're a writer. Fucking write. Even that little Bieber wanker's got a book out, and his head's empty as my fucking bowl.

Here's your fucking weed. Maybe I should call a shrink. Have someone hypnotize me, that'll dredge something up.

That'd be a laugh, eh, watching a deaf guy get hypnotized. What, are they gonna caption that shit for you?

Hardefuckinhar. Pour me a JD and coke, would you, Lemmy?

You want a toke, too? Might help knock loose a few memories.

Weed makes me uncomfortable.

Maybe that's a good thing.

• • •

I eventually got used to wearing my hearing aids at school, taking them off when I got home. It seemed unnecessary for me to wear them at home—I was used to my family's voices. I wore hearing aids to appease the outer world; it was for appearances. Inside my own home, I wanted—and received—the freedom to be myself.

My parents deserve a lot of credit. They never forced me into anything I didn't want to do, and they were patient with me. We spoke a few times about the possibility of cochlear implants. They explained that it would involve inserting mechanisms into my head that would boost my hearing even further.

"It'd be like the Terminator," my dad said. "Half-man, half-machine."

My mom gave me a picture showing a young boy with what looked like a brown bottle cap poking through his blond hair. A grey wire sprouted from the cap. I grimaced. Hearing aids made me stand out enough—I didn't want to stand out even more.

"I don't wanna do this."

"Why not?" my dad said.

"It's weird. I don't like it."

"It could really help you, Adam," my mom said.

"I don't want help. I just . . ."

We were sitting at the kitchen table. I picked fuzz off the swivel chair I sat in and looked toward Sooey, our cat, who lay on the living room floor sprawled out in a sunbeam.

"I don't like it," I said.

My parents looked at each other. Mom pulled away the picture.

"Are you sure?" she said.

"Yes."

I got up to sit down beside Sooey. She rolled over and mewed, and I scratched behind her ears.

Even at that age I saw my deafness as a kind of firewall protecting the contents of my head. I didn't want my head invaded by virulent sound. Diminished noise levels were crucial for my sanity.

• • •

In Grade Three, I attended Roy Wilcox Elementary School. My best friends, Colby Carter and Kieran Thistle, were in the same class. I never had difficulties communicating with them: they were both as loud and as zealous as I was. Colby and I often played hockey together or watched television—"Go go Power Rangers!"—and Kieran and I played video games and went on hikes with his dad into the woods surrounding Kitimat.

During one such hike, Mr. Thistle led us into a clearing near a pond. He used his walking stick to separate the weeds and cattails. He jabbed his stick into the ground. "Boys! Come here!" he said.

Kieran and I traipsed over to him.

He held up his hand, on which rested a large mosquito. "Watch, watch its belly."

The mosquito stuck its needle into his skin; slowly its belly swelled with blood. It glowed in the daylight like a tiny ruby.

"Only the female mosquito can extract blood," Mr. Thistle said.

I think he went on to discuss the mosquito's anatomy. I hardly listened. I watched the mosquito. I couldn't believe Mr. Thistle would voluntarily let the mosquito bite him. Mosquitoes were thieves, tiny bandits, nothing more than useless pests. I'd never thought twice about killing them, and Mr. Thistle was letting this one rob him of his blood.

"Yach!" I said.

Just as Mr. Thistle stopped speaking, I smacked the mosquito, leaving a bloody smear on his hand. Kieran snorted, and we both laughed. Mr. Thistle frowned and wiped his hand on his pant leg.

This method of engaging or rather disengaging became a habit: I'd ignore what other people said while focusing on my own musings and ruminations. Most of the time it did little harm—at least that I could see. I was mostly ignorant of the impact my deafness had on other people, and I spent much of my childhood thinking I was blameless. I probably bothered or frustrated the people whose words I missed and might have—shit, most likely—caused a few people to resent me.

In one instance, ignoring the words of another left me bruised and bloody.

One summer day Mom took my brother and me to our friend Rory's house on Bartholomew Street, a house we'd eventually buy. Rory, Taylor, and I all had what were called "rattails," hairstyles modelled after the New Kids on the Block, whose song "Step by Step" played on the radio all the time.

While Mom left to do a few errands, Rory and his mother invited Taylor and me into their backyard, where they kept their ATV. Rory, my age but a good two inches shorter than me, climbed onto the ATV and drove tidy curls around the backyard, weaving between the kiddie pool and his little sister's playset.

"Adam," his mother said, "would you like to try?"

"Yeah!"

After Rory demonstrated how to use it, I got on—no helmet, no pads. Rory's mother, who was pretty and had thick black hair and deep olive skin, explained several things to me: probably where the brake was and how to accelerate and how to steer and where the brake was and where I should go and where the tricky patches were and where the brake was. I didn't hear her. I was too excited. I wanted to plow around the yard and crush one of Rory's toys and maybe even try a trick or two. And if I succeeded maybe I could drive it on the street and race a few cars. If Rory could handle it, why couldn't I?

"You understand, Adam?" she said.

"Yeah-huh!"

"Okay, so now you—"

I gunned the engine. I plowed straight into a wire fence, flipping over the bars and landing in a snarl between the fence and the ATV. I gasped and cried. A piece of the fence had snapped out and stabbed me just below my left ribs. Rory's mother rushed over to me and helped me inside, where she cleaned my wound and put a large Band-Aid over it. When Mom came back, she took me to the hospital, where they determined that the fence piece had scraped my lung. "Just scraped, though," the doctor said. "Nothing really to be done, nothing to worry about."

There is a difference, of course, between not hearing because of deafness and not hearing because of the jamboree of excitement brewing in one's imagination. But for me the distinction between the two has become blurred. My deafness allows me to retreat into my imagination, and my imagination has become a bizarre and beautiful garden because of the greenhouse effect my deafness has had. Although I haven't used an ATV since that day more than twenty years ago, I still have a habit of ignoring people and focusing on my own imaginings, though I like to think I've become more aware of the frustration, embarrassment, and resentment it's caused.

• • •

"Mrs. Cumberland?"

My Grade Three teacher glanced up. We all sat on the floor in a circle around her, and she sat in her blue chair reading us *Charlie and the Chocolate Factory*. Across the classroom, Roy Wilcox's special education liaison—I want to say Linda—stood in the doorway.

Mrs. Cumberland adjusted her glasses. "Yes?"

"May I borrow Adam for a few minutes, please?"

I put my hands to my mouth.

Mrs. Cumberland smiled at me. "Go ahead, Adam."

I looked at Linda, then at Mrs. Cumberland. "What about the story?"

"You can catch up when you get back. It's okay."

As I stood up, Kieran made a face at me. I made a hissing sound at him.

"Come with me, Adam."

Linda led me down the hall to a small room. On the table were two electronic units, one with a microphone attached and another with what looked like an incomplete headset. It had a single wire that divided into two wires capped with small receivers.

I stopped. "What's this? I said I didn't want implants."

"This isn't an implant," Linda said. "This is an FM system. Did your parents not speak to you about it?"

They had, but I'd been watching the Canucks play at the time and had ignored them.

"So," Linda said, "you hook your hearing aids up to this, and your teacher will wear this, and you'll hear her voice directly. Okay? Here, take out your hearing aids, and let's try it out."

I sat down at the table and turned off my aids. "What do I—"

"Just take out your hearing aids," she said. "Then you insert them into these boots." Linda inserted one of my hearing aids into one of the receivers, then handed me the other receiver. "Try it."

I inserted my aid into the boot. It fit perfectly. "Do I put them on now?"

"Yes, go ahead."

I put my hearing aids back in, pulling the unit closer.

Linda's voice was muffled. "See this little switch? You just push it upwards, and make sure you're on the same channel as this other unit. Channel eight."

I turned on the FM unit; a green light glowed. I switched my aids back on.

Linda turned on the microphone unit and held it to her mouth. "Can you hear me?" Her voice gleamed. It was as though someone had taken it and buffed it with silver polish.

"Wow," I said. "Say something else."

She smiled. "Is it clear?"

I grinned.

After lunch, Linda gave Mrs. Cumberland the microphone to wear. She stood at the front of the classroom looking down at the microphone and holding her arms out as though a cockroach had jumped on her.

"Adam? Is this okay?"

I nodded.

My classmates studied her and me. "What is that?" someone said.

"It's something that will help Adam hear," Mrs. Cumberland said. "His ears work differently than yours and mine do, and he needs this to hear me."

I smiled in gratitude. It was a relief not to have to strain myself trying to read my teacher's lips all the time. I used the FM from Grade Three all the way to

Grade Twelve. I was able to follow almost everything my teacher said.

Not to say there weren't difficulties. The FM's battery would sometimes fail in the middle of a lesson, emitting a sound like a turning signal, and I'd have to interrupt the lesson to let the teacher know. I clipped my unit to my pocket hem or belt until the day I received a fanny pack and began walking around the school like a pensioner on vacation. My classmates would sometimes steal the microphone and cover their mouths and whisper obscene things. About a week after I first got it, Kieran and a few other students lifted the microphone from Mrs. Cumberland's desk and walked into the corner by the bookshelf and started saying "Can you hear this? Shit! Can you hear this? Asshole! What about this? Dickhead!"

The worst hiccup occurred during a math lesson. The teacher—out of respect, I won't say which one—was leading us through a number of problems on the board when she said she had to leave the class for a few minutes.

"Keep working on the problems in the textbook," she said. "I'll be right back."

She put down her chalk and walked out of the class-room. While the rest of my fellow students put their heads down and went to work, I heard my teacher's footsteps clicking down the hallway.

"How are you?" she said to someone passing by.

I heard a door open, followed by a familiar clank. Then a pronounced click. Then a rustle. Then splashes began filling my ears.

I sat Norman Rockwell–straight in my seat and stared forward, listening to my teacher on the toilet, too horrified to think about turning off my unit. When she returned to the classroom, I couldn't look at her directly or answer questions for a week.

My FM system became a symbol of my position in the world. It connected me to the hearing world while also separating me from it: I could hear what was going on, but no other kid wore a fanny pack or had direct access to the teacher's voice or had grey wires fastened to his head. No other kid had to speak to the teacher before and after every class. No other kid was compelled to sit at the front of the room, in prime teacher's pet real estate. I felt both self-conscious and privileged.

• • •

My dad worked for CN, just as his dad did before him and just as my brother would several years later. We moved to Kitimat because he'd been transferred, and in the summer of 1994 CN transferred him again, this time to Prince George.

That was a painful summer. The Vancouver Canucks had lost to the New York Rangers in the Stanley Cup finals, an occasion I'd lamented by running out of my Auntie Jeannie and Uncle Dan's house on Eagle Street and hopping on my bike and crying and screaming while pedalling as fast as I could down Nalabila Boulevard. I'd also developed a major crush on a girl in my class, Monica, and felt like I was abandoning the love of my life. To top it all off, I'd be leaving behind my beloved Auntie Jeannie and Uncle Dan, my cousins Ryan and Michael, my friends, my teachers, the place I learned to play hockey, the community to which my family and I belonged. I pleaded with my parents to the point that they actually created a list of pros and cons for staying in Kitimat, with "Adam happy" being on the pros side. But Dad had to transfer, so in July 1994—shortly after everyone saw O.J. Simpson drive his white Bronco through

Los Angeles—we left a small coastal city of about 11,000 for a city of 75,000.

• • •

You're gonna talk about it now, right?
   Not yet.
   What the fuck you waiting for?
   Not the right moment.
   Any moment's the right moment to talk about music, man. And you're a deaf guy. Who wouldn't want to hear a deaf guy talk about music?
   I'm not fucking Beethoven. I'm not composing symphonies here.
   Your hair's wild.
   I'm tired of hearing about Beethoven. We need new stories, new icons. And, hey, at least my hair colour is real. Unlike yours.
   I will hit you, you know. I'll stick my picks between my knuckles and fucking whale on you.
   Sorry.
   You keep saying music was a big thing in your life.
   It was. Is. I love music.
   What kind of shit did you listen to?
   All kinds of stuff. Zeppelin, Bryan Adams, Boston, KISS. Especially KISS, my dad's a diehard KISS fan. Bob Seger, Dr. Hook, Def Leppard, Poison, Meat Loaf, Randy Travis, Tracy Chapman, Eagles, Heart, Alannah Myles, Dire Straits. My brother and I used to sing "Money for Nothing" all the time, but we'd always get the lyrics wrong, like "Money for nuffing and steekoh-fee!"
   No Motörhead?
   Motörhead came later. You gonna pass the JD?

No Elvis? No Buddy Holly or Little Richard? No Beatles?

No Beatles in our house.

Gimme that bottle. What kind of fucking upbringing is that?

Yeah, I know. One of my earliest and happiest memories was coming—I was about three or four—and we were coming home from my Uncle Wade's house in Ashcroft. It was dark, about nine p.m. I thought my parents were gonna put us to bed, but my dad walked into the living room and turned on the stereo and played Cheap Trick's cover of Elvis's "Don't Be Cruel." And we all started dancing. My mom went to turn on the lights, but my dad said, "Leave them off." We danced and jumped around in the dark, holding hands and singing, my brother and I belting "Don't be crude" as loud as we could. At the end, we all fell on the floor laughing.

Dancing in the dark. Springsteen would be proud.

That's what my wife said when I told her that story.

But seriously, man. No Beatles?

No. I thought I'd forgotten that memory. Jesus.

Rock n roll, man. Roll n roll.

• • •

Taylor and I enrolled at Glenview Elementary School, a short walk from our pink mobile home on Taft Drive. A few days before school started, my parents and I met with my Grade Five teacher, Mrs. Martinson.

"It's lovely to meet you, Adam," Mrs. Martinson said in a thick yet pleasant Hungarian accent. I usually had difficulty with accents, but I could understand her easily, so I loved her. I showed her how to use the FM system, which she viewed with great curiosity, asking about the channels and the batteries and which position was best for the microphone.

Despite the preparation, I went into the classroom anxious. Understanding Mrs. Martinson was one thing; relating to my classmates was another. Although many of them were pleasant, I sensed an edge of discomfort. I felt like an iguana tossed into a flock of ducks: the class had already formed cliques, and my presence disrupted them.

At school most of the boys my own age were indifferent toward me. If we hung out, it was more out of convenience or obligation than anything else. They were there, I was there, friendship was provisional.

The older boys challenged me. About a month into the school year, a few Grade Sixers walked up to me during recess. One of them, Clayton, appeared to enjoy pushing me around. He wore a frayed ball cap and a No Fear T-shirt and appeared to wear black eyeliner. He slapped me on the shoulder.

"Hey. You're deaf, right?"

"Yes."

"Can you read lips?"

I looked at the others standing behind him. They watched me with malevolent curiosity, as though I were a bullfrog they'd rigged to blow up.

"Yes."

"Tell me what I'm saying."

He mouthed the words *fuck you*.

"Eff you," I said.

He slapped me on the temple. "The hell you just say to me?"

The others stirred and grinned.

My hands shook. I breathed deeply to stifle my tears. "That's what you said." I didn't like the whimper in my voice. It was like a cockroach scuttling across my vocal cords. I bit my lip.

"What am I saying now?"

He mouthed the words *you fucking faggot*.

"You. . . ."

"What'd I say?" He stepped closer to me and mouthed them again.

I shook my head. "I don't wanna say it."

"What's wrong? Did you miss it? Are you dumb?"

"No!"

"Are you afraid?"

I sobbed. "You fucking faggot!"

The others shouted. Clayton grinned. Some of the kids playing hopscotch glanced over at us. One of them said, "I'm telling!"

"He said it!" I said, pointing at Clayton.

"Shut up!"

Clayton pushed me. I stumbled backward. He pushed me again, driving his shoulder into me like a rugby player. I fell down into a dense patch of wet grass.

"Keep your fucking mouth shut," he said.

The recess buzzer sounded—a flat, dispiriting sound. I stood up and brushed the grass from my pants and watched the other kids file back inside. I stayed still. The world seemed to uncouple beneath my feet. The school, coloured a vomitous pink and drab at the best of times, seemed to shrink and darken; its walls looked like they were made of cardboard, as though the school was part of an elaborate stage set. I missed Kieran and Colby and Monica. I missed Roy Wilcox and Auntie Jeannie and Uncle Dan and Ryan and Michael. Prince George was too grim, too ugly.

"Hey, you!"

I looked up.

The recess monitor waved to me. "Come on back in!"

I took a step forward, testing the ground. A pebble shifted under my shoe. I stopped.

"Come on, let's go!" The woman waved again.

I whined—again the cockroach traipsed across my vocal cords. I slowly walked back into the school.

During our first year in PG, many times I came home from school crying, and it frustrated me because I couldn't solve my problems on my own. I didn't like receiving help—I still don't—and I would get these terrible feelings as if little stones were clogging my synapses. Being new exacerbated the usual difficulties I had with my deafness: I had trouble adjusting to the new voices and facial expressions. I would often get mixed signals and react in the wrong ways; also, most of my classmates hadn't met a deaf kid before and didn't know how to respond to one. That winter, during a game of chess, I put a classmate in check, then told her that she couldn't take my piece if I had her in check—which of course was wrong, but I thought I'd heard Mrs. Martinson explain that rule.

"Are you sure?" my classmate said.

"Yes!" I said. "You can't move. And if you're in check like this, then I win."

My classmate, a gentle and kind girl, let her king down. It was a bullying thing for me to do, but I didn't want to admit I was wrong. I was competitive, and I didn't want to appear inadequate—or, really, I was competitive *because* I didn't want to appear inadequate. I feared inadequacy above everything else.

• • •

One day in October or November 1994, I was sitting in the living room looking at an empty plant hook in the ceiling. I'd had a difficult day at school: Clayton and his myrmidons had tested my Sign Language skills with some obscene gestures, sticking their fingers between their legs and asking, "Is this a sign? What about this? And this?" I stared at the hook. I thought, *What if I hanged myself?* I imagined taking some rope from the shed and dangling from that hook or from a tree outside.

The thought scraped my head clean. It was a revelation because I saw that I had that power. I could exercise that amount of control. Why not remove myself from life, with all of its toothy edges and booby traps for which I was never prepared? Why not leave a shadow for Clayton and my classmates to deal with rather than my bruisable, scratchable, breakable body? Why not avoid all of the potential misunderstandings and strained relationships? It seemed so simple.

A short time later Mom and I had a conversation about suicide. I can't remember if I brought it up, or if it began because of something else that happened, but I remember asking if she'd miss me if I killed myself.

"Yes," she said. "It'd break my heart, and your dad's and your brother's, and everyone else in our family."

I recall feeling relieved that someone would miss me. I also felt arrogant, as though I wanted to see how much their hearts would break. Would there be a big funeral? Who would come? Would they cry? For how long? Would they put a notice in the paper? Which picture would they use? Who would speak at my funeral? What would they say? Where would they bury me? Would my death have a long-term impact on anyone?

"You're not thinking about that, are you?" Mom said.

"No," I said. "It was just something I saw on television."

The thought quickly became a comforting fantasy. It was like writing a brutal and hateful letter but never sending it. I poured all of my poison and filth and out-rage into the prospect, imagining my own death doz-ens of different ways; then I plodded onward, usually unharmed but sometimes not. Sometimes, in my late teens and early twenties, I sent only part of the letter, not the whole thing.

The thought still comforts me.

• • •

About halfway through my Grade Five year, my speech started to degenerate. Mom noticed that my voice had taken on a hollow sound, and Mrs. Martinson grew concerned, saying that she didn't want me to lose my speech, that she wanted me to have the greatest chance of success in the future. My parents, Mrs. Martinson, and I met with a speech therapist, and soon he and I began meeting on a regular basis.

My therapist, Mr. Zhao, was a kind and patient man but boring. Synapse-slowing-down-to-tar boring. He spoke with a measured, monotonous voice calibrated for the sole purpose of being heard by and setting an exam-ple for young deaf kids. He always had a set plan and had little tolerance for deviations. We would do lip and mouth movement exercises and watch parts of videos; when I realized I wouldn't get any satisfaction by saying words that weren't on our curriculum or by asking him strange questions, I spent most of our sessions nodding my head and retreating into my imagination. I didn't want to speak like him. I wanted a dynamic voice, my own voice, a voice that could barrel through the air and make any room I spoke in seem like an arena, a voice that pinged people on the ear and forced them to listen, a voice that could thwack people's funny bones and crack their hearts in two, a voice like Rodney Dangerfield's or Marie Fredriksson's or Krusty the Clown's.

One week Mr. Zhao gave me a list of words to take home. I had to stand in front of the mirror every day and recite the list from top to bottom, watching the way I formed each word and correcting myself when necessary. The evening of the first day I stood before the bathroom mirror and began reciting the list. I've always had difficulty with my "r" sounds and with rapid shifts in consonants, and the list was loaded with such words.

"Regg-ee. Rrr-rrr-rrreggie. This'll. Thist-uhl. This-tell. Thistle? Thleh."

I put the list down and watched my mouth.

"Who are you? Ace Ventura, pet detective. Ay. Sss. Ven. Chur. Ah. Pet. Dee. Teck. Tive."

I leaned forward.

"Whatdya—what do you know about Ray Finkle?"

I took a deep breath.

"Kocker syle sticker—pbbbbbt!"

I shook my mouth out, wagging my tongue.

"Soccer-style kicker graduated from Collier High June nineseeneventystix Stetson Uni—University honours graduate class of nineteeneighty."

I breathed deeply again.

"Soccer-style kicker graduated from Collier High June nineteenseventysix Stetson University honours graduate class of nineteeneighty holds two en-cee-double-ay diwision—division one wec—wecords—records. Dammit."

I kept practising the speech, my favourite moment from *Ace Ventura*. Over the next two weeks, I practised it hundreds of times until, on a rainy but brilliant day, *"Soccer-style kicker graduated from Collier High June nine-teenseventysix Stetson University honours graduate class*

*of nineteeneighty holds two en-cee-double-ay division one
records one for most points in a season one for distance
former nickname the mule first pro athlete to come out of
Collier County one hell of a model American!"*

Once I could do that speech three times in a row, I
switched gears. "Coming out the defensive zone, Boo-
weh—Bure to Linden, pushes it back to Bure, Bure
steps awound—around the defendeh—defenderrrr, on
a bweakaway—scores! What a move by Pavel Bure!"

I tossed the list Mr. Zhao had given me and walked
around the house chanting lines from *Dumb and
Dumber* and *The Lion King* and *Halloween 4* and *The
Simpsons*. I sang songs by Bryan Adams and imitated
Jim Hughson's play-by-play narration. I became more
familiar with my voice's habits. I can't hear myself speak,
but I can feel when something's off, when I'm mumbling,
or when I'm mispronouncing something. I calibrated
my speech according to feeling rather than sound; in
other words, I located the nest of cockroaches waiting
to skitter across my vocal cords and found a pesticide
that could keep them away.

Whenever a voice appealed to me, I imitated it. I
still do. I absorbed all of the voices of my childhood,
and by dialing my attention to their cadences and their
imaginative use of words I improved my speaking voice.

• • •

My family has had many pets—dogs, cats, rats, turtles,
and tarantulas—and I've never felt more at ease than
when I've been playing with our dog or lying on the
couch with our cat on my stomach. I love all animals.
Part of it is their remarkable ability to love uncondi-
tionally. Part of it is their complete and comforting

lack of inhibition, of not caring whether or not they look silly. The greatest part is I never have to worry about misunderstanding animals. I don't have to read their lips or ask them to repeat their barks or meows or worry about missing subtexts. Animals speak with more clarity and simplicity than humans ever will, so when one of my pets dies it leaves a scar on my soul.

In the spring of 1995, our dog Gino ran away. Gino was a mix of Boston and Maltese terrier, a black-and-white bearded ruffian. He was getting older by then—my family had had him since the year I was born—but he was still as bouncy as ever, chasing Sooey around the house and humping her whenever he could.

Gino had a habit of running away down the street and barking at passing strangers, but he always came back. This time, though, he stayed away. We searched the neighbourhood for him, calling his name and asking people if they'd seen him. Because of his age, we were worried that he might have died.

Later that day, shortly after Dad came home from work, Gino traipsed down the driveway and up to the front door.

"Gino! Good boy! What a good boy!"

We petted him—he winced. He lurched rather than walked. His spine looked as though it'd been hauled two inches upward, and he wheezed and made small gulping sounds. Someone had beaten him.

After consulting with the vet, my parents excused Taylor and me from school the next day and had Gino put to sleep. They brought Gino home in a box. Wrapped in a blue blanket, he rested on his side, tucked in the deepest of sleeps. Mom asked if there was anything Taylor and I wanted to put in the box with Gino; I put one of his favourite treats into the box. I kissed his head.

Dad had dug a grave for Gino in the backyard, framing the grave with two-by-fours. Mom, Taylor, and I watched and cried as Dad gently lowered Gino into the grave and replaced the dirt. He'd built a cross for him, on which we hung his brown collar.

About a week after we buried Gino, Taylor was playing in the yard, and Terence, the older boy who lived in the trailer behind us, walked past. He lived with his dad, who had loud parties every weekend; my dad always had to ask them to turn down their music and stop shouting. A few times Taylor and I found beer bottles along our fence.

Terence slowed down as he walked. He had a pale face with a smattering of freckles and a thin slit of a mouth and purple circles beneath his eyes. In my memory, his face had an almost plastic sheen. He looked at my brother and smiled.

• • •

Every month or so our class would receive the Scholastic Book Club flyer. The flyer was a collage of stories and characters, and I loved thumbing through it. One day when I brought it home, Mom asked to look at it and spotted a book called *Helen Keller's Teacher*.

The cover depicted a middle-aged woman wearing dark glasses trying to calm a little girl wearing a bright blue dress. Even though tears slipped down the girl's face, her expression was stoic. The girl stared ahead though not straight at me. The whole scene was awash in golden light.

Mom talked to me about the book. She told me who Helen Keller was and suggested that we order the book. When it arrived, I didn't read it. I was more interested in the other two books I'd ordered: a *Calvin and Hobbes* book and a novel about a kid whose parents were vampires. The Helen Keller story made me bristle. I didn't want to be the deaf kid who read about another deaf person. I was afraid that by reading the book I'd somehow sink deeper and deeper into deafness, and I didn't want to. I also didn't want stories that preached determination or set good examples or inspired me to overcome obstacles. I wanted characters that belched national anthems and broke windows and sang dirty songs. I wanted boisterous narratives that frolicked and twisted across vast, menacing landscapes. I wanted to laugh. I wanted to gasp. I wanted to roar. I wanted entertainment.

My attitude extended to friendships. Even though Prince George was a bigger city with a more diverse population, I didn't know any other kids who were deaf or hard of hearing. My parents tried introducing me to a few: one day, about a week after another hearing test, Mom invited a boy with cochlear implants to our house. He immediately discomfited me—those black cyborgian antennae, those wires curling out of his head, those blinking red lights. He threatened my territory. I wanted to be the only deaf person in the house—in the world, really. I resented his openness, his ease, his comfort with himself. I searched him for flaws, for reasons not to befriend him; he made me feel inadequate. I dismissed the things he liked and clung to what I saw as my hearing superiority, like an upwardly mobile plebeian in a Dickens novel afraid of associating with the wrong people. He asked me questions I don't remember. I mentally blocked him out.

After he left, Mom asked me if I wanted to hang out with him again. I said no. He probably said the same thing to his mom.

I was never fully at ease with the hearing kids in my class either. When I reached Grade Six, things became so difficult that my teacher, Mr. Lawrence, organized a meeting, or intervention, at which three of my friends—or kids I hung out with—and I had to talk about why we didn't get along. We sat in a semicircle, the three of them—Angus, Sam, and Dirk—across from me and Mr. Lawrence in between us. Angus, Sam, and Dirk scanned the floor, looking for distractions. They were as uncomfortable as I was.

"I understand that Adam often feels left out," Mr. Lawrence said. "It seems strange to me why you don't get along. Can any of you explain it? Do they leave you out, Adam?"

"Yes," I said.

"We don't leave him out," Sam said. Dirk and Angus nodded. "It's just . . . he gets confused."

"It's because I'm different," I said. "I'm not, maybe, fully part of things. They gang up on me."

"Are the three of you uncomfortable with Adam's deafness?" Mr. Lawrence said.

"No. Well, no, but yeah," Angus said. "We—well, he kind of uses his deafness as an excuse."

Sam and Dirk nodded. I scoffed. Angus explained that during lunchtime we often played a game called Red Butt (we called it Red Ass) behind the school. We'd throw a tennis ball against the wall, and if you dropped it you had to run and touch the wall before someone else threw the ball. If you beat the throw, you were safe. If you didn't, you had to stand facing the wall while someone threw the ball at your ass. Whenever we played Red Ass, or tag, or soccer, I'd bend the rules in my favour and later claim I'd never heard anyone state the rules.

Angus was right, though I never said so. I tilted my head back, draining back tears.

"All right, listen," Mr. Lawrence said. "I'd like the four of you to agree to something. Adam, you need to listen more closely, okay?"

"What? How?"

"You need to figure that out for yourself. It's something you all need to work out. And the three of you need to learn to be more tolerant. You have to meet each other halfway. Understand?"

"Sure."

I bristled. Mr. Lawrence dismissed us, and we all walked out together.

"That was screwed up, wasn't it?" Sam said.

Although we all agreed, it was clear they still thought of me as separate from them. I had the same thought.

If there was one place I did feel at ease, it was at the hockey rink. Hockey not only gave me years of unbridled glee but also ended up giving me a way to communicate with kids my own age. I couldn't make many friends at school, but I made plenty through hockey. I spoke the game's physical language, its grammar of space and line and motion—you pass to me, I pass back to you, we score on them, and we prevent them from scoring on us—and I used that language to relate to my teammates. Scoring a goal or making a strong defensive play meant I'd communicated successfully, so I consistently pursued that sort of communication.

In December 1995, a Kitimat team came to Prince George to play in our annual Christmas tournament. Although we were in the house league, the Kitimat team was a rep team, made up of the best atom-age players.

Everyone on the team wore jerseys and matching socks and jackets and jester's toques in the colours of the Florida Panthers. Many of my old friends were on the team, including Colby Carter. My team, which wore black, played them in the round robin. Although our team was strong, and featured a future NHL draft pick, the Kitimat team was structured, skilled, and speedy. We lost 5-1.

I cried during the handshake. I felt like I'd lost twice. It was too much knowing I would have been on their team if we'd stayed in Kitimat. And, just to make it even more difficult, the Kitimat coaches selected me as my team's player of the game. I accepted the medal through a skein of gratitude and longing.

After that game, Mom, Taylor, and I went downtown to the Holiday Inn to visit with the Kitimat players and their families. When we arrived, the players were splashing around in the hotel pool, with their parents sitting nearby.

"Adam," Mom said. "Do you wanna go change and jump in the pool?"

She held up a plastic bag with my swimming trunks in it. I looked at the Kitimat players laughing and shouting among themselves. The loss hummed in the back of my mind. I felt the way Wayne Gretzky must have when he first walked into Edmonton after being traded to Los Angeles. I didn't feel as connected to the Kitimat kids. Although we all spoke hockey, I wanted to speak hockey with my Prince George teammates Rasmus and Holden and Peter, with whom I shared a common goal.

"No," I said. I sat by the edge of the pool with Mom and Taylor. Colby asked me to jump in and splashed water on me. I said no.

Kitimat went on to win the tournament, but more than a year and a half after moving I'd finally found a community of friends on the ice in Prince George.

• • •

Now?

Yes, now.

About fucking time. How'd you start?

Like just about every other drummer. I was eleven, and I started tapping out beats on the table and the dashboard and the car seat and on books and VCR tapes and really any surface that was available. When I did my homework, I'd sit at the desk and listen to "Detroit Rock City" and play the beat on the edge of the desk. My parents hated it. So they suggested, as much out of love as out of a desire to strangle me, that I learn to play the drums. I got this instructional video—David Eagle's Drum Basics. You know him?

Maybe. Sounds familiar.

I bought a practice pad and a set of drumsticks and played with that for a while. Little paradiddles and such. Later I bought a bass drum pedal and anchored it to a laundry basket 'cause I didn't have a drum kit. It helped me get used to playing with my feet, but I knocked the bottoms out of two baskets. Mom wasn't happy.

You can hear the drums, right?

It's in my range of hearing, yes. When a guitar goes into the high notes, I can only hear the picking, not the notes themselves. Drums, I hear everything. When I was twelve, I saved up money from my paper route and bought a set of black Westbury drums. I put them in the shed behind the house and played for hours and hours.

You think you play the drums just to show you can do it? You know, like, ooh, look what the deaf guy can do.
That's not my mindset.
You think your deafness kind of—I don't know—helps you play the drums? Like that Scottish one, I forget her name. Plays with bare feet.
I don't know. I just wanna enjoy myself and play the music I love. Lot of metal. Hard rock. Complex, driving beats, like Slipknot, Mudvayne, Iron Maiden, Tool, Disturbed, Lamb of God, Slayer, Metallica, Papa Roach, Korn.
Motörhead?
Sometimes, though Motörhead's drumming isn't always complex or interesting.
Fuck you, man.
Well, it's true, isn't it? You're the centre of the song, not the drums.
My drummer's a fantastic drummer.
I'm not denying that, but you could've given him more room to create and show his talent.
You telling me how to run my band?
No. I'm sorry.
Are you scared of losing your music, like of not hearing it in the future? Did you hear me?
I heard you. I don't wanna answer that right now.
Why not?
Just. Not right now.

• • •

From a young age, I loved to draw. I'd sit at the kitchen table with my pencils and markers and sketch pictures of Godzilla and Peter Venkman and Slimer and the Teenage Mutant Ninja Turtles and He-Man and Batman and Robin and all of the other icons of my childhood. The chemistry of pencil and paper and the composition of images came naturally to me, and being a child with an overheated imagination I sought every outlet.

When I discovered *Calvin and Hobbes* at age nine, I found more than a boisterous, imaginative companion; I found a potential career path. My drawings became more directed; I added dialogue and thought bubbles to my characters, and when I was twelve or thirteen I started creating cartoons of my own, ripping off ideas from *Calvin and Hobbes* and *The Far Side* and *Garfield* and *Archie* and *Herman*. I created a character called Dunderhead and worked zealously, Dad and Taylor occasionally contributing puns and ideas. Taylor gave me the idea of a cartoon about the cow that jumped over the moon. He said I should draw an astronaut stepping in a pile of cowshit. I added the dialogue bubble "That's one small step for man, one giant— oh, my god, what did I step in?" I kept all of my cartoons in a Harley Davidson file folder in my desk; my desktop itself was swathed in ideas and works in progress.

By the time I was in Grade Eight and attending Kelly Road Secondary School, I'd created another character, a pig called Oinker. I was proud of Oinker; he combined the gluttony of Garfield with the shit-disturbing whimsy of Calvin. I read (and delivered at six in the morning) the *Prince George Citizen* newspaper, and when I got home I always read the comics section as I ate breakfast, enjoying the stories while scoping out the competition and envisioning my own work among them.

A short time after I created Oinker—in March or April 1998—I was in PE class in the middle of a wrestling lesson. We were just getting ready to pair off and scuffle when my mom appeared at the gym door. She called to me; being fourteen and about to wrestle, I was quite embarrassed. I sidled over to her.

"Do you want to meet Ben Wicks?" she said.

I didn't quite understand what she was asking me. Ben who? Behind me, my classmates were taking off their shoes and preparing for their matches.

"No," I said.

Mom's face slackened. "Yes. Come on. We're going."

"Wait. Ben Wicks?"

"Yes!"

"Aha! Yes. Okay."

While Mom spoke to my PE teacher, I left to change. Ben Wicks was one of Canada's most prominent cartoonists, with an incisive political instinct as well as a sniperish sense of humour. As Mom explained on the drive downtown, Wicks was in Prince George to give a talk, and Peter Godfrey, the kind editor of the *Citizen* to whom I'd recently—perhaps overweeningly—submitted cartoons, had arranged for the two of us to meet.

We arrived at a hotel on Central Street. I was wearing jeans, a white Reebok T-shirt, and an alien necklace. Godfrey and Wicks were talking by a potted tree; Godfrey spotted me and gestured to Wicks. Wicks wore a dark patterned sweater and dress pants.

"Ben," Godfrey said, "this is Adam Pottle. He's a young cartoonist whose work I've been reading."

"Hello, Adam," Wicks said in a soft Cockney accent.

We shook hands—I stifled a gasp. His handshake could squeeze tears out of Hades.

My mom had brought along my file folder of cartoons. Wicks and I spoke for about ten minutes, during which he looked over my work.

"I think this is wonderful, what you are doing," he said. He talked about his approach to the art, how he thought of it like storyboarding for a film. At the end, he shook my hand again. A *Citizen* photographer captured our meeting, and we were featured in the paper the next day.

A week or two later Godfrey asked to meet with me. Mom and I drove to the *Citizen* building downtown, and he invited us into his office.

"Adam!" he said. "Please, have a seat, both of you."

Mom and I sat down. Godfrey smiled at us. He was one of the last true newspapermen who believed in the power of ink and newsprint.

"Adam, I've been reading your cartoons," he said. "Thank you for sending them to me. How would you feel about publishing *Oinker* in the *Citizen*?"

I looked at Mom, whose face reflected my own surprise. I laughed.

"Really?"

Godfrey chuckled. "We'll give you a spot in the paper every Saturday. Sunday-strip style—you'll have three rows of panels. You get them to me by five o'clock every Thursday, and we'll pay you forty dollars per cartoon."

"You're—you're gonna pay me?"

"Absolutely."

I laughed again. Mom and Godfrey did too.

"How's that sound, Adam?"

"That sounds—sounds great!"

Godfrey shook my hand and Mom's hand, and I left that meeting wondering how I could be so lucky. A professional cartoonist at fourteen years old! What was next? *Vancouver Sun*? *Toronto Star*? *New York Times*? Worldwide syndication? *Oinker* merchandise?

Oinker debuted in the *Citizen* on Saturday, May 9, 1998, on the first page of the arts section. That first strip featured Oinker at an Alcoholics Anonymous–like meeting, called Slobaholics. Oinker takes the podium and admits his addiction to mud. The joke was weak, but having a crowd of slobs shout "HI, OINKER!" seemed to be the best way to introduce the character.

After a month or so, I became bored with the strip. Mom and Dad kept reminding me to finish my cartoons so they could drop them off in time. Once, I was rushed—homework and drums and street hockey—and handed Mom a cartoon that was less than professional.

"Adam, no," she said.

"What's wrong with it?"

"Look at this." She shook the paper. Scabs of white-out fell from the page. "You need to go back and do this over."

"I don't want to." My voice had a whine that I, for once, intended.

Mom's eyes darkened. "You've been given a great opportunity here, Adam. Kids all over the world would love to do something like this. Do you want Mr. Godfrey to receive it with all these mistakes? You want him to think you're unprofessional?"

"Ugh. No."

"Okay. Now go back downstairs and draw it over again."

I took the page and went into my bedroom and took my time redrawing the strip; like Calvin begrudging his father's attempts to build his character, I begrudged Mom's lesson on professionalism.

Oinker continued until December, when cutbacks at the paper forced Godfrey to scrap the cartoon.

• • •

At school there was a special ed room where I picked up my FM system every morning. Other Deaf and disabled students worked in that room, but I never did.

I just grabbed my headset and microphone and left. I never felt any camaraderie with them. I never made the effort.

The usual problems persisted: my FM battery would die in the middle of a lesson, or my teacher would forget about the microphone when he or she went to the lounge (but not the bathroom, thank Christ), or my fellow students would steal the microphone to whisper obscene or flirtatious things. One time in my Grade Nine science class, a girl's voice tinkled through my hearing aids.

"Adam."

I looked up. My teacher, Mr. Arnold, didn't have the microphone.

"Adam."

I glanced to my side.

"Back here!"

I turned my head. Two rows behind me I saw my classmates Alicia, Cameron, Nancy, and Nicola gathered around the microphone. I blushed. The girl holding the microphone, Nicola, laughed.

"Can you hear me?" Nicola said.

I nodded.

"Do you have a girlfriend, Adam?"

I shook my head and whispered, "No."

"Why not? You're such a stud."

I blushed more and looked at the floor. The girls laughed. I didn't like the attention but at the same time I did.

"Is there anyone you like?"

"I don't know," I said quietly. I looked over at Mr. Arnold, busy marking papers.

Cameron took the microphone. "Come on, who is it?"

"No one," I said.

"Is it someone in this classroom?"

"No!" I hissed.

"Who is it? You can tell us."

"I don't—"

I turned off my unit and faced forward. Their questions upset me; I didn't know what to do. I'd never experienced flirting anywhere, much less in the classroom. To me, the classroom was for working, and flirting—however well meaning it might have been—violated my boundaries.

One time my FM system had to be taken away for repairs, and I had to get through the day with just my hearing aids. I was in my Grade Nine social studies honours class with Mr. Putnam, the relentless coach of the junior girls' basketball team. He asked me a question about the nineteenth-century expansion of Canada; I didn't understand him. He asked again. I still didn't understand him. He stepped forward and asked again. I ducked my head and started to blush. I said I didn't know. He persisted. My classmates watched. I felt their pity. I said I didn't want to answer the question. Mr. Putnam asked again, extending his arm over a map of Canada and sweeping it westward.

"They went west?" I said.

"Good," Mr. Putnam said.

The class moved on. I kept my head down. Since then, I always feel hot barbs whenever I ask people to repeat themselves.

At that time, in addition to dealing with the usual teenage baggage, I was trying to untangle a snarl of new emotions. My parents had separated just after Christmas in 1998, and Taylor and I had to choose which parent to live with. Both Mom and Dad were looking at houses in Prince George, and they'd take us along, asking us to imagine our bedrooms, our living rooms, where we'd eat dinner. We chose to live with Mom, who, after living in an apartment for six months, bought a house on Willowdale Drive.

While Mom worked, Taylor and I managed the household. I had two or three good friends the first few years of high school, but from Grade Eleven onward my social circle exploded. Mom started dating soon after she bought the house, and having her away a lot helped. Our house became a popular spot for the so-called misfits, kids who liked Monty Python, kids who understood the social value of marijuana, kids who loved *Fear and Loathing in Las Vegas*, kids who harboured grave suspicions of the government, kids who after half a dozen beers could resolve the Israel-Palestine crisis, kids who acted, kids who played music, kids who came from outside Canada, gay kids, unsure kids. No deaf or disabled kids, though. I was the only one.

Not only did my social circle explode in Grade Eleven, but also my imagination found its anchor, its true outlet. In English that year, I had a teacher named Dr. Ivan Carridon. A big, bald, boisterous man, his eyes darting from behind his glasses, he'd grown up in post–Second World War Germany and worked as an orderly in a mental institution before getting his PhD. He'd tell us stories about the people he'd met while working in the institution: "There was once a paranoid man there, he'd been there for a few years. And every time I passed him he'd tap my arm and say, 'You know they're after me. They've been after me for years. But that's okay, because I'm not really here!'" Carridon was the ideal high school English teacher, vulgar one moment and philosophical the next. He was a grenade in a microwave, an IED in a dragon's mouth: a thousand different ideas and stories were always queued up at the front of his brain, waiting to burst out.

In the first week of class, Carridon performed Edgar Allan Poe's "The Tell-Tale Heart," holding his can of Diet Coke, his free hand wobbling with excitement as he steadily led us into the narrator's failing sanity. Once he finished, I knew I had to try to produce that effect myself, and shortly after I began writing stories and poems.

One of my writing assignments in Grade Eleven English was to take a familiar fairy tale and create a "true" version of it. Carridon had told us the true story behind Cinderella: after marrying the prince, she had ordered that her stepmother and stepsisters be tortured by being forced to dance in white-hot iron shoes. I decided to tell the true story behind the Three Little Pigs. My title: "The Three Little Pigs: A Tale of Prostitution." I named the three little pigs—really three prostitutes—after three snotty female schoolmates. The wolf became a john who delighted in the pigs' huffing and puffing; instead of the wolf blowing houses down, the pigs blew the wolf. Carridon loved my story so much he read it aloud to the class, wisely eschewing the huffing and puffing. The three schoolmates I'd satirized never knew, or if they knew they never retaliated, or if they knew and were upset by it—if they walked past my locker and shot barbs at me—I never heard them.

The first few original pieces I wrote were derivative crap. Like many beginning writers, I imitated my first influences: Poe, Stephen King, John Steinbeck, George Orwell, Dylan Thomas. One story, though, I was quite proud of, called "Gargoyle Alone." It's about a gargoyle that sits atop a church and watches everything that happens in the streets below him. When terrible things happen—a man is robbed and shot, a child is hit by a car—the gargoyle experiences great pain, and because he can't move he can't do anything about it. Only after being struck by lightning and left in pieces on the sidewalk below does he experience relief.

• • •

One night in spring 2001, my friend Rasmus Bellagard, with whom I'd played hockey in atom years before, took me to a party in downtown PG, which we called the Bowl. It was, in Richard Van Camp's words, "pure monkey house trauma." Every room was clogged with drinking teens. I didn't drink, but I gladly served as Bellagard's designated driver, in itself a reliable source of adventure. I had one rule with him: "Don't fuck with me, or I'll drop you off at the wrong house."

Just after midnight, the cops showed up, and everyone scrambled. Bellagard got to my car ahead of me, and I ducked in after him. I gunned the engine and whipped around the corner—right into a police checkpoint. Three or four cop cars cut off the street to ensure nobody drove drunk. A policeman walked up to my window. I rolled it down and waited for him to say something.

"Hey!" The policeman smacked my door. "Did you hear me?!"

"Pottle!" Bellagard said. "Give him your licence!"

"Shit!"

I scrambled to get my wallet and gave the policeman my licence. I waited another minute. The policeman's head was above the window, and I couldn't read his lips.

The policeman smacked my door again. "What is this?! Come on!"

"Pottle! Give him your registration!"

"Shit! Here."

I opened the glove compartment and gave the policeman my registration.

He lowered his head. "Step out of the vehicle."

I looked at Bellagard. He had a curious expression, somewhere between a grimace and a smirk.

I got out of the car.

The policeman waved me to the rear of my white '91 Cavalier. "Why didn't you answer me?" he said. "Have you been drinking?"

"No! I'm part deaf in both ears. I can't understand you if I can't read your lips."

Revelation and mild guilt crisscrossed his face. The cop shook it off and looked at my licence. "You haven't been drinking?"

"No."

The cop studied me. "Can you open the trunk for me, please?"

I glanced at Bellagard, watching us. Before we'd left his house that night, he'd put a case of Pilsner in the trunk. He'd taken a few six-packs into the house, but there were still a good dozen beers left. Being seventeen, I didn't understand that I had the right to refuse the cop. I walked over to the trunk, looked to the sky for help, and opened it. My jack, tire iron, and jumper cables were there like always, along with an empty beer case. The cop reached inside and turned everything over. I thought I saw a flush of anger—his attempt to retake control had flopped. In the car, Bellagard was laughing and squirming in his seat.

The cop handed me my licence and registration. "Get the hell out of here."

I got back into the car and drove past the checkpoint, leaving the wash of flashing blue lights behind us.

When we cleared the street and got onto the main road, Bellagard patted my shoulder. "That—that was beautiful, Pottle," he said.

"Where's the beer?" I said.

Bellagard giggled. He peered over his shoulder, then reached into his wide-leg jeans and brought up a can of Pilsner. Farther down his leg, I could see the outlines of the eleven other cans. We drove to his house, laughing all the way.

When my brother got into high school, he soon fell in with what we called the "Necks," guys who wore scuffed-up ball caps and jean jackets with iron-on patches who drove lifted trucks and spent their time playing rugby, destroying property, and creating new ways to get drunk. They were the bane of Kelly Road Secondary School and the local police, and Taylor, gifted as a guitarist and rugby player, occasionally invited them to our house, usually when Mom was out.

One night, after a school dance, I invited some of my friends over. Mom was away for the weekend. It was February 2002; Willowdale Drive was stifled with snow. We heard that the Necks wanted to come over, so we turned out all the lights to make it look like no one was home. Ten sixteen- and seventeen-year-olds hunkered down in the living room, sitting on the carpet quietly sipping their Pilsner and Smirnoff. Half a dozen Necks announced their presence by driving their snow-mobiles through the neighbours' yards. At first they saw the lights out and went away, but then they came back when the lights were on. My brother invited them inside, assuring me he could control them. I scoffed. Whenever his friends came over, he always tucked himself in his room and played guitar, disregarding everything else.

Within a short time, the Necks were pouring beer into our dog's water dish and flicking the lights on and off. I told them to stop. My friends timidly nursed their drinks. Bellagard and my other friend Marty came up to me and said, in subdued voices, "Help is always three numbers away."

I went into Taylor's room. Half a dozen Necks surrounded him, watching him play Metallica's "For Whom the Bell Tolls."

"Tay, can you come here for a second?"

"Just a minute."

"Now."

Some of the Necks chuckled. "Tay? Like Gay Tay?" They laughed.

Taylor stood up and walked over to me. I pulled him into Mom's room.

"The hell?" he said.

"I don't want these guys here. They're fucking shit up."

"They're fine. They're not hurting anything."

"They poured beer into Molly's dish, and I don't want them in the garage around my drums. They—" I heard a dry thud. "What the fuck?"

I ran out to the garage. Four Necks stood around my drumkit, the same one I'd bought five years earlier. One of them had kicked in my KISS bass drum head, a rare piece of memorabilia Dad had given to me. I walked up to the drum. A shred of the drum head stirred from the wind generated by my footsteps.

"Who the fuck did this?" I said.

The Necks glanced at each other, smirking.

I huffed. "That's it. All of you get out." I picked up a golf club and held it over my head. "Get the fuck out!" I chased them out of the garage, smacking the club on the concrete. I ran back into the house. "Everyone! Everyone get out! *Now!*"

My girlfriend, Bethany, walked up to me and took my face in her hands. "Are you okay?" she said.

"No! I'm not okay! I need everyone to leave before I bash in someone's skull." Everyone watched me. "Why are you standing around! Get the hell out!"

It was around 2 a.m. by the time everyone had left. I paced around the living room, saying "Fucking hell, fucking hell," and opening and closing my fists. I had so much anger and no way to spend it.

I turned to the computer and wrote an email about what had just happened, and at the end I wrote "I want the heads of the following individuals," and I named the Necks who were in the garage at the time. I ended the email with "Death to the Jean Jacket!"

I sent the email to as many people as possible, asking them to spread the word. My intention was to put a scare into the Necks. I hated that they kept getting away with destroying other people's property.

The email spread—through the school and through the city. People in Ontario replied to it. Someone added the subject line "Kelly road hicks are gonna pay! holy shit you gotta read this." I'd uncorked a bubbling hatred. People—not just other high school students—were adding their own stories and promising similar retribution.

A few days later I was called into the principal's office. It was lunchtime, and as I walked through the common room someone threw an orange peel at me. I brushed it off and kept walking.

The principal, Mrs. Cunneyworth, invited me into her office. I'd never been in trouble before, and given the severity of the email I anticipated getting suspended or even expelled. I tried to block my parents' faces out of my head. I wanted to go to university, and I'd jeopardized that.

"Have a seat, Adam," Mrs. Cunneyworth said. "How are you doing?"

"Okay," I said.

Mrs. Cunneyworth's window looked out onto the Kelly Road staff parking lot. Past the parking lot was the pocket between school property and the woods surrounding the property, where kids went to smoke and socialize. Some of them were on the way out, others on their way back. A few of them peered in at me and slowed down. I bit my lip.

"I invited you in here," Mrs. Cunneyworth said, "because there's been an issue with an email that's been circulating around the school."

"Okay."

"An email you wrote."

I dropped my eyes to the floor. The voice of the Soup Nazi from *Seinfeld* shunted through my mind, but instead of *No soup for you!* it said *No school for you!*

"Has anyone tried to harm you?"

I looked up. "No."

"Has anyone called you or emailed you?"

Yes. "No."

Mrs. Cunneyworth nodded and adjusted her glasses. "If anything does happen, if someone threatens you with violence or says something harmful to you, I want you to come to me. We'll deal with it. Understand?"

"Yeah."

"Anything that happens."

"Okay."

She looked me in the eye.

I waited. "Is that it?" I said.

"That's it. You're free to go."

Mrs. Cunneyworth stood and shook my hand. She smiled a little—I thought to be reassuring.

The next day, while I was sitting at the computer reading the latest batch of emails—some threatening, some jubilant—the doorbell rang. Taylor went to answer it. I heard a male voice ask my name.

Taylor turned to me. "Adam?"

I walked over and saw a police officer standing there.

"Are you Adam Pottle?"

"Yes."

"We have concerns about an email that's been going around."

"Okay."

"Has anyone called you or tried to harm you?"

"No."

"Have you heard any threats or anything about other people being hurt?"

"No. Am I being charged?"

"No. I'm just here to talk to you about this to find out if you've heard of anything happening. If you do, please make sure you call us."

He gave me a card.

"I will," I said.

The policeman left. I wasn't charged with uttering threats. I wasn't suspended or expelled. The orange peel was the most threatening thing that happened to me. After thinking about it for a while, I realized that the school and the police were grateful to me. I'd done something they'd been unable to do: scare the Necks.

The Necks episode was my first true lesson in the potency and volatility of the written word. It can scare people. It can incite violence.* It can spread quicker than bloodlust through a gang of skinheads. It has power the supposed authorities don't have. But I had to figure out a way to use that power in a more positive and productive way.

• • •

It's like you're avoiding it.

I'm not. It's just who cares?

I wanna hear about girls. Action, you know. What, were the girls you dated manatees or something?

No. They're just not part of the narrative.

Did you date deaf chicks? Did you sign with them? How'd you ask them out?

I—I don't really know. I just kind of fell into relationships. I'd find out a girl liked me, then go out with her for a few months. Never dated deaf girls in school.

How'd you talk to them?

Just like you and I are talking. And they sometimes passed me notes or talked to me online. But the best conversations were in bed. My high school relationships were always physical. I understood that. I understand skin contact and sex. I understand pleasure, the rhythms of the body. I think my deafness has helped in that way.

You had a lot of girlfriends?

No. I had like two or three girlfriends in high school.

You had a favourite?

My wife.

She go to high school with you?

---

*   I later heard that some of the Necks had been chased by kids from other schools carrying chains and baseball bats. I don't know if that's true. I hope it's not.

No, but I know better than to say anyone other than her is my favourite. Know what I mean?
Not at all, man. Never been married.
You been in love?
Sure, man, a thousand times over.

• • •

My suicidal thoughts became more urgent in the years following my parents' separation. I spent hours visualizing my own death: bowing beneath a homemade guillotine, hanging myself from a bridge, locking myself in the car and leaving it running in the garage, swallowing a bottle of pills, slicing open my carotid and sinking into what I thought would be death's velvety embrace.

One evening when I was sixteen or seventeen and had the house to myself, I cranked up Slipknot's "Purity" and shut all the blinds and turned the living room into a one-man mosh pit. I headbanged. I threw pillows. I shoved and overturned furniture. I smacked my head into the wall. I screamed the lyrics at photographs of my family and friends. I listened to the song two or three times; then I took a butcher knife from the kitchen and walked down the hall and stood in my bedroom doorway. I held the knife's handle against the moulding and angled its tip toward my heart. I nodded to the drum track still rolling in my head. I gripped the handle. The sharp tip poked through my shirt. I winced and arched my back to distance myself. I groaned. I hated that I didn't have the strength, and that made me want to do it even more because I felt weak. It seemed so simple: stick it through the flesh. Flesh isn't strong. Muscle tears easily. Think like you're cutting through a roast. One solid thrust, a few gasps, and you're done.

I threw the knife aside and punched the wall and went out to the garage and sat down at my drumkit and played "Purity" and "Surfacing" and the dozen other Slipknot songs I knew. As I played, the faces of my friends and family whisked past, staring at me. I hit my drums as hard as I could, trying to beat them away. I imagined my schoolmates watching me, expressions of disgust and discomfort on their faces. My brain churned with a choking brew of depression and teen angst cut with something else—the trenchant fear that I couldn't relate to anyone, that no matter how hard I tried I'd always be separate, always be alone.

During the last song—I think it was "Liberate"—I cut my finger on the edge of my snare drum. I kept playing. Blood whipped up and down my kit. The pain soothed me and drove me forward—I played faster than I'd ever played. I shrieked the lyrics. I beat my drums harder so they'd cover my voice. I stood up and hit my crash cymbal with my forehead. I finished the song with a scream, and with my bloody finger I drew my initials on my snare skin. Then I sat there for a moment, wiping the sweat from my eyes. I removed my headphones and listened to the night. No cars passed. No dogs barked. No kids shouted. It was as though my drumming had left a crater of silence in its wake. I dropped my drumsticks and cried.

• • •

It's never worth it, man. You know, people say Hendrix would've rusted out if he'd lived, but they're full of shit. Greatness is greatness, and Hendrix would've gotten greater and become a living legend, you know, like Little Richard and Paul McCartney and Stevie Wonder.

And you?

When I was alive, yeah.

Jimi Hendrix didn't commit suicide, though. And Kurt Cobain, Cobain was already great. He would've become greater if he'd lived.

Probably. Actually, I don't know. Maybe it's best that he died.

Wait, what?

A lot of his impact, his influence, comes from the fact he shot himself. Any kid picking up a Nirvana record for the first time will, you know, read Cobain's music through his death. It's a terrible fucking thing. He and the world weren't built for each other.

You could say the same about Hendrix.

Hendrix got into the wrong drugs. That was his problem. If he'd taken speed that night instead of downers, he'd have lived. He could've become the king or greater than the king. You have to create your place in this world.

Cobain tried.

He failed. He gave up before he could finish. Left his little daughter behind, man.

I'm not sure this is the best thing for me to hear.

It's reality. But you'll be fine. You're a good kid. You won't be great like Hendrix or Hemingway, but, you know, you'll do some good things.

That's reassuring. Do you wish you were still alive?

Can't make music when you're fucking dead, can you? Can't get laid. Can't see the people you love. Can't make people happy or make yourself happy.

Is that what music's for? Is that what art's for?

What the fuck else is it for?

• • •

Up until Grade Eleven, I'd played both hockey and volleyball, and with college looming ahead I had to choose one sport. I'd always played house-league hockey, and many of the high-level hockey players in Prince George drank, took drugs, and skipped school. High-level hockey also cost a kidney and half a liver, and the parents, who'd invested thousands of dollars trying to turn their kids into NHL prospects, were animals, deluded hyenas who barked at their kids and tore into their opponents. I attended one game between two bantam rep teams, standing beside my friend Peter Woodley, who played for one of the teams but was injured. After the home team took a penalty, many of the parents started berating the visiting player who'd goaded the home team.

"You little shit!" they screamed. "Get off the ice! You're a fucking joke!"

The captain of the visiting team grinned. He glided past the crowd and made a gesture like he was jerking off at them.

The parents nearly jumped over the glass. "I'm gonna get you, you bold little fucker! I'm gonna get you!"

I looked at Peter. "Dude, is it always like this?"

He smiled and nodded.

"How do you stand this?"

"You just play. You deal with it."

In addition to avoiding such a toxic environment, there were more opportunities for me as a volleyball player. After my Grade Ten year, I was chosen to play at the BC Summer Games, and I had a better chance of snagging a volleyball scholarship than a hockey scholarship. Although it broke my dad's heart, I decided to focus on volleyball.

My teammates were rollicking, funny, perverted, hardworking, competitive guys who sang obscene songs and took delight in swatting each other's asses, but our coach, Archie, was an immature, bullheaded prick. He knew the game and had a relentless drive to win, but he had no idea how to properly manage a group of teenagers; in particular, he had no idea how to talk to deaf teenagers.

During the season, which ran from September to December, we'd play a tournament just about every weekend, and we'd often play in enormous gymnasiums, which meant that there were usually other games going on at the same time as ours. Balls bouncing all over the place. People shouting and cheering. Whistles blowing every five seconds. My deafness helped me block out distractions, but Archie demanded that I wear my hearing aids every game. I could have said no, but he had an abysmal temper. One time after a loss he spent ten minutes berating us within hearing distance of a gym full of people. He told us how much our performance pissed him off, and in the middle of his tirade he punched a door and split a knuckle. So I did what he said, even though I couldn't concentrate worth a damn.

In 2001 we took a road trip to Kelowna to play in a tournament at what was then called Okanagan University College. In addition to our game, three other games were being played.

In the first set, my team, the Kelly Road Roadrunners, was leading by three or four points, and the other team was serving. Along with my teammates, I crouched down, ready for the ball. Just as the player served the ball, I heard a whistle. I stood up straight and looked to the referee. The referee was watching the ball cross the net. The ball was coming toward me. I took a cursory bat at it but was too late. The ball touched down. Point for the other team.

My teammates were irate. "What the fuck, Pottle! Wake the fuck up!"

I tried to explain that I'd heard a whistle. The referee looked at me like I'd grown a third eye. I realized that, because of my hearing aids, I'd heard a whistle from the other side of the goddamn gym. That play ended up being pivotal: we lost the set. I turned my volume way down and didn't look at Archie. From across the court, I could feel the steam spurting from his ears.

I thought working with him would make me a better player, and to a point it did. I learned different aspects of the game and became more positionally sound, but he sucked the joy out of the sport. I never got within sniffing distance of a volleyball scholarship, though when I graduated I did receive two bursaries, along with two academic awards: Top Writing Student and Top English Student.

• • •

During my last year of high school and my first year of university, I volunteered at the Prince George Brain Injured Group. My mom had worked there since I was in elementary school, and she'd sometimes come home and tell us stories about the survivors—what they did, what they said, how they'd acquired their brain injuries. When we were younger, Taylor and I, little shits that we were, roared at her imitations of the people she worked with. Mom would make twanging sounds or speak as though her mouth was full of radiated slugs. She didn't intend to be mean. She thought that we wouldn't understand, that we'd be discomfited by the survivors, so she used humour as an inlet, as a way of inviting us into their stories. I wish we'd known better.

A few times Mom took us with her to meet the survivors, Bailey and Jonah and Elma and Darnel and Chase and Laverne and many others. We'd sometimes go on outings to the lake or meet them at the office or group home. I didn't want to go—I couldn't laugh if I knew them. I wondered if they were fully aware of their conditions. I wondered if they felt betrayed or angry. A few of them yelled or screamed or threw objects across the room. Sometimes the men got into fistfights. I remember Mom telling me about a time she drove Elma around to run errands. Elma had curly dark hair and glasses, and her eyes were like Salman Rushdie's: sly, no matter the situation. At one point, Elma and Mom were on the freeway in Prince George, driving over fifty, and Elma tried to open the car door and escape. Mom had to pull her back in and struggle with her while keeping the car steady.

When Taylor and I visited with the survivors, I felt an empathy I didn't want to feel. Did people laugh at me the same way I laughed at them? Did people see me as less intelligent, less able, less human?

By the time I began volunteering, my discomfort had dissipated. In addition to being beautiful people, the survivors were bottomless sources of story. Darnel always got into fights, yet he also carried himself with a sweetness punctuated by his enormous toothless grin. Jonah acquired his brain injury by falling out of a tree when he was young, and he was unable to swallow— doing so would have been lethal for him—so he always had to spit in the sink or a pop can. He had to receive food through a tube in his belly button, which broke my heart because he loved baking peanut butter cookies but could never eat them.

The survivors knew I was deaf, and they made sure they looked at me when they spoke. Whenever I saw

Darnel or Jonah or Bailey in the street, they always shook my hand and asked me how I was doing, and I did the same. When I was younger, I always wondered whether they really recognized me or whether what I said made sense to them, but as I worked with them I saw the difference between the heart and the brain. When the brain doesn't function the way it should, the heart takes over; it knows what matters. It didn't matter whether or not the survivors were aware of their conditions. What mattered was that they kept surviving. Their acceptance of themselves and their ability to carry on rubbed off on me, and I began to grow more comfortable with my deafness.

• • •

I began writing my first real novel when I was eighteen and enrolled at the University of Northern British Columbia. I still used an FM system and still experienced unique situations: once, when the professor left the room and forgot she was wearing the microphone, I heard her order a double-double at the Tim Hortons around the corner from the classroom. Much more pleasant than the splash of urine in the toilet or fatigued complaints in the teachers' lounge.

Titled "The Greatest View," after a song by Silverchair, my novel centred on a young Deaf woman named Madison who, after the deaths of her parents, goes to a music school for Deaf and hard-of-hearing people. The school is situated in Jasper and uses innovative techniques to teach the students music. Madison works through her grief by becoming a vocalist, refining her harmonies, and building friendships with her schoolmates.

The one thing that makes me proud about "The Greatest View" is its 400-page length. I loved the weight of the printed manuscript in my hands. That weight reflects the work habits I developed, particularly my discipline. By working on the novel every day for six or seven months, I created a bivouac around myself. It didn't matter if I worked on the book for five hours or thirty minutes—I had to be there every day. It was difficult. At home we had only one computer, which sat along the wall between the kitchen and living room. There was no door to close, so to maintain my bivouac I had to fend off my mom and brother whenever they needed the computer. My deafness helped me construct the walls of my bivouac; I could ignore or pretend to ignore them when necessary.

Other than that, "The Greatest View" is a narrative hardly worth saving. The plot reeks of Harry Potter, the deaths of Madison's parents arouse little empathy, and Madison herself is dull and whiny. The book also exposed the huge hole in my imagination: I had no idea what being part of the Deaf community is like. Although I resisted the idea of research, and snottily thought my own experience and imagination were all I needed, I eventually learned I had to do my homework if I was to write honestly.

I sent the novel to half a dozen publishers across Canada, thinking the book's length and my young age would warrant at least a little consideration. None of the publishers bit, though, and I didn't write about deafness or disability for another four years.

In the meantime, I continued to write novels that, like "The Greatest View," were justifiably rejected: a Dickens-like story about a man on death row who wants to learn to read before he's executed; a thriller about a serial killer whose murders are strikingly similar to those depicted in a crime writer's books; a historical novel about gold prospectors working in and around Barkerville.

Although my novels sucked, I did manage to publish a short story in an online journal called *Scroll in Space*. Run by a UNBC professor, *Scroll in Space* didn't pay anything, but it did provide many authors with their first publications. My story "The Whale" details a young boy's experience finding a beached orca in Kitimat. The boy, who has recently lost his dog, studies the whale and listens as a group of men discuss what to do with it. The men are drinking and soon start cracking jokes about catapulting the whale and carving it up. Their conversation frightens the boy, who gets on his bike and rides away.

A crucial part of writers' development is the discovery of their subject matter. Writers develop the ability to turn a phrase and construct a narrative, but then they must use those skills in a directed manner. As I worked my way through my bachelor's degree, I ended up publishing two more stories in *Scroll in Space*. "The Shame of Not Knowing" focuses on an older married couple. The wife is diagnosed with cancer and begins to express herself more freely, surprising and at times troubling her husband. "Casual Spillage" features an old woman looking through a box of photographs. The pictures trigger random memories linked by her regret about always hiding her thoughts and feelings. The story ends with the old woman dropping the photographs and evacuating her bladder.

Physical vulnerability. Freedom found through bodily difference. I was getting closer. I wanted a subject that could be both entertaining and idea driven, a Pandora's box stuffed with neon lights and elastic walls and steel cables and bone music that could reveal humanity's best and worst qualities.

• • •

The Cadillac Ranch used to be a hot nightspot in Prince George. Every weekend, bands would take the stage and play shitty covers of Toby Keith and Travis Tritt and Alan Jackson and Hank Williams, along with the occasional original tune. Anyone who drove down Second Avenue at 1 a.m. could hear the drumbeats spurting out the door, wet and harsh, like a humpback whale's flukes splashing on an ocean of Pilsner. The club closed in 2009 after its staff members were arrested for hawking drugs.

Four years earlier, on a warm October night, a few friends and I went to the Cadillac Ranch—or "Caddy," as locals called it—for drinks and dancing. I'd been reluctant to go. I didn't drink, and I preferred moshing to dancing; also, being deaf made it extremely difficult to communicate in a rowdy environment. But I wanted to have a good time with my friends, and for my friends a good time meant going to the Caddy.

The Caddy's neon green sign flashed above us as we entered. The band inside was butchering AC/DC's "Money Talks." *Easiest fucking beat in the world*, I thought, *and this drummer can't keep time.*

The club was packed with dancers and drunken singers—a regular Friday night in Prince George. The band looked like a collection of insurance agents, all of whom wore polo shirts and no doubt wore white briefs and proudly displayed Stephen Harper's picture on their desks.

My friend Aruna grabbed my arm and pulled me toward the maelstrom. She pointed toward the bar, where the lineup was ten deep.

"I'm all right," I said.

She spotted a table nearby. I read her lips: ". . . over there! . . . our seats!"

I walked to the table and sat down while Aruna and the others went to get drinks. The band mercifully ended "Money Talks" and began playing "Sweet Home Alabama." *Oh Jesus,* I thought. I glanced around. A group of women scuttled onto the dance floor and began doing their best impressions of marionettes plugged with angel dust. A man and a woman in their forties took their beers onto the floor and toasted the band and began singing along; the man didn't notice he spilled beer onto his shoulder. The lead singer's voice was like Foster Hewitt's on helium. The green and blue stage lights whirled and tilted in a rhythm all their own.

By the time the singer cut into the first chorus, my breathing had quickened considerably. I clenched my fists. People at the next table drained a round of shots. Those at the bar had turned around and raised their hands and shouted the chorus. More and more people were coming into the club. My hands trembled. I sweated. I stared at a dent in the dance floor. I lifted my arm from the table; it was sticky. I felt like I'd found my personal corner in hell.

I glanced over at Aruna. She was four spots back from the bar. The drumbeat, still off time, clashed with my own speedy heartbeat. One of the dancing women grinned and waved at me. Her eyes were black in the aimless blue light. I stood up from the table and fumbled my way through the crowd and strode out the door down the street around the corner into my white Cavalier.

1. BECOMING DEAF

I locked the door and sat there. An electrified cockroach bucked and quivered and clawed in my chest. I leaned forward with my head against the steering wheel, trying to control my breathing. It was like trying to wrestle smoke into a box.

I saw an oil change receipt on the floor. I snatched it and pulled a pen from the glove box and started scribbling furiously.

YOU'LL ALWAYS BE ALONE YOU PATHETIC COCKSUCKER NO ONE WILL GET IT YOU'RE A WORTHLESS DEAF SON OF A BITCH FUCKING DEAF BOY DEAF BOY DEAF BOY SHOVE A KNIFE IN YOUR THROAT YOU HAVE NOTHING TO CONTRIBUTE TO THIS WORLD YOU HAVE NOTHING WORTH SAYING NO ONE IS LISTENING TO YOU NO ONE CAN RELATE TO YOU NO ONE WILL LOVE YOU YOU ARE SUPPOSED TO BE ALONE YOU WILL ALWAYS BE ALONE YOU SHOULD JUST FUCKING DIE YOU WORTHLESS USELESS GOODFORNOTHING PIECE OF SHIT

I crumpled the page and threw it in the back. I bit the pen hard enough to leave teeth marks and tossed it away too. I bit down on the steering wheel. My heartbeat thumped against the strong rubber between my teeth.

Someone knocked on my window. I gasped and looked up and saw Aruna. I rolled down my window.

"Adam? You okay?"

I wiped my forehead. "I think I'm gonna go home."

"Oh. Are you sure?"

"Yes."

"Okay. Well, . . . we'll see you later."

When I got home, I took a steak knife from the drawer and went into the bathroom. I took off my shirt and started cutting my arms and chest. The knife had a serrated edge—I slowly pulled it across my skin, slicing through my forearms and biceps. I made cuts in neat rows and cuts in random slashes. Bumps of blood swelled through the cuts. The pain thrilled me. Relieved me.

Afterward, I washed and treated the cuts and looked at them in the mirror. They blushed out like crimson letters in an alien yet familiar alphabet. Their power frightened me. They seemed to communicate more in a few brisk strokes than I ever could after years of writing and studying English.

. . .

You're not one of those, are you?

One of what?

Those ignorant motherfuckers who buy into that myth and think their mental illness is the key to their creativity. Because it's bullshit. Suffering doesn't make you creative. You're creative because you're creative, and that's it.

I was lonely and scared and angry, but I didn't want to lash out or hurt anyone or drive anyone away, so I took it out on myself.

Just rage out on the drums, you know. Break a window. Get drunk and fight someone. Don't hide in your bathroom whining "Poor me, I'm deaf." Just get it out. Go to a rock concert.

It seemed the best idea at the time. I'm not proud of it. I fucking hate it. It's the oldest trope in the book—the self-hating disabled guy.

Makes me angry when smart people like you do stupid things like that. Especially with metal fans, you know, 'cause it's like you're saying that the music isn't enough to get you through. Metal fans know how to punch through the bullshit. *They save everything up for the concert floor, and then they're fine.*

I didn't feel I had a choice. That's what mental illness is, the diminishment of choice. There've been days when I can't tell where my deafness ends and my mental illness begins. One exacerbates the other. On days when I misunderstand my wife or my friends, on days when I'm in an environment where communication breaks down, my deafness and depression conspire, intertwining like barbed wire, ensnaring me, choking me, cutting me off. Hopelessness is often a default position for me.

Pour me another drink, will you?

Do you believe that life is meaningless?

You're talking to me right now, even though I'm fucking dead.

I read somewhere that Churchill's depression helped him see the threat that Hitler posed. I try to see the practical side of things. I've spent so much time seeing the hopelessness of life that it's become beautiful to me.

Fuck off with that shit, will you? Next you're gonna tell me Jim Jones was a brilliant leader.

Hopelessness is truly sublime. It clears your head through erosion. It's exhilarating, because if you have no hope you're unshackled. It's true freedom. If you see the world as a void, you can scream whatever you want. That's beneficial for a writer, especially one who sits in a corner writing things that people don't wanna hear. You're unburdened by expectations. You see the pettiness, the smallness of life. As a deaf person, I'm seen as especially insignificant. Because of that, I work hard to reach an equal measure of insignificance.

That's funny. We're all insignificant, but we need to be equally insignificant. Well, all you alive fuckers are small. I'm bigger than life now. Literally.

Smallness is good for a writer. I just wish I didn't always feel small.

They got pills for that.

I've done pills.

I mean Viagra.

Heh. You dirty old man.

Have you ever had help? Counselling, weed, speed, weekend in a brothel, backpack to Tibet?

Done the counselling. I don't really do drugs, and I don't do that self-discovery bullshit. I'm not Elizabeth Gilbert. If I'm gonna solve this, I'm gonna solve it right where I am. I think I still harbour ableist attitudes. I still expect myself to conform. I'm a straight white guy. I carry privilege into every interaction. But my privilege ends as soon as people start talking. I'm not an equal participant in the conversation, but I try to carry on like I understand, because I know most people don't have the patience, and I hate imposing on others.

That's manning up, isn't it? If you need something, you gotta ask people.

I know.

If you could get rid of your deafness and depression, would you?

No. Because otherwise I wouldn't know that panoramic hopelessness that drives me to connect with others and allows me to see the rusted gears that move the world and frees me from artistic expectations. Deaf and disabled people—not me, 'cause I'm not much of a role model—but other Deaf and disabled people are beacons of hope, because every day they work toward a better world that will welcome them. You're right that suffering doesn't make you creative. Suffering just makes your creativity more urgent.

• • •

In September 2006, I began my master's degree at UNBC. I initially wanted to write about postmodernism and Miriam Toews's novel *A Complicated Kindness* but soon abandoned the idea. Postmodernism wasn't sexy enough, and as good as Toews's novel is I doubted my ability to squeeze an entire thesis out of it. I knew I wanted to study Canadian fiction, but if I was going to study multiple works I had to find a common theme.

In a previous class, I'd written a paper about Ann-Marie MacDonald's novel *The Way the Crow Flies*, which has a disabled character named Elizabeth. She is a minor character, and I started thinking about how disabled and Deaf characters typically hover in the backgrounds of stories. I found a book called *Enforcing Normalcy* by Lennard J. Davis, which introduced me to the field of disability studies. I found other books by Rosemarie Garland-Thomson, David T. Mitchell, Sharon L. Snyder, and Shelley Tremain. Their ideas about disability—its literary history, its disruptive potential, its narrative richness—tore open an entire sphere of my brain. I started exploring the way deafness and disability are portrayed in Canadian fiction, focusing on contemporary writers: Rohinton Mistry, Frances Itani, Ann-Marie MacDonald, Guy Vanderhaeghe, Lori Lansens, and Arley McNeney. I found that deafness and disability consistently arise in Canadian fiction, but hardly anyone seems to notice them. I also found that, even though Deaf and disabled people make up the largest minority in Canada, they are seldom prominently featured in our literature. The gaps in Canadian—really, worldwide—literary history are enormous.

In their book *Cultural Locations of Disability*, Mitchell and Snyder talk about how the Nazis treated disabled people during the Second World War. The gas chambers used to exterminate Jewish citizens were first used in psychiatric hospitals in Hadamar, Hartheim, Bernburg, Brandenburg, Grafeneck, and Sonnenstein. The victims were told they would be able to shower, then asked to undress and step into the shower room. The metal door was sealed behind them, and a psychiatrist turned on the gas. Later the victims' gold teeth were removed. Under the euthanasia program, which Hitler called Aktion T 4, more than 275,000 people with disabilities and mental illnesses were murdered.

I couldn't believe I'd never heard of these atrocities. Why didn't my history teacher talk about this in high school? Why didn't people talk about these things whenever they spoke about the Holocaust? Why wasn't there a *Schindler's List* or *Diary of Anne Frank* or Primo Levi or Elie Wiesel telling the story of these people?

I pulled out a piece of paper and started writing a poem about a man sent to the euthanasia clinic in Hadamar. Promised a cure, the man and his companions are stuffed into the shower room, where they hear "the monstrous groan of iron pipes." As the man and his companions slowly die, he thinks, "No one else will probe into our lives. Nothing will grow from our deaths except the usual twinges of mourning. No new tree will emerge from our ruins, no fiery bird will arise from our ashes. We lay scattered, life unworthy of death. The story of the mass the same and different."

The poem, eventually titled "Aktion T 4—October 1939," was my first serious attempt to write about disability. Over the next several weeks, I wrote dozens of poems. I wrote about the survivors at the Brain Injured

Group. I wrote about deaf people, blind people, people
with intellectual disabilities, paraplegics, and dyslex-
ics. My imagination, which I can't shut off at the best
of times, churned out image after image, phrase after
phrase, story after story. I felt like I'd discovered a new
drug, one that caused constant synaptic explosions and
stretched my heart wide enough that just about anyone
could nestle inside.

PART 2

DEAFNESS AND THE WRITER'S VOICE

ON LANGUAGE

Throughout literary history, writers from foreign backgrounds have seized the English language and shoehorned it into their own idiosyncratic rhythms, creating unique and dazzling works. Józef Korzeniowski, a young Polish boy, did not learn English until his twenties; in his thirties, he reinvented himself as Joseph Conrad and became one of the world's greatest writers. Jean-Louis Lebris de Kérouac grew up speaking French in a French Canadian community in Lowell, Massachusetts, but several years later, after learning English, he rechristened himself Jack Kerouac and published the American classic *On the Road*.

Although English is my first language, I, like the heavyweights who came before me (though I am nowhere near as talented as they are), have an uneasy relationship with it. My deafness defamiliarizes language and makes me experience words in a different way: I write according to how words feel rather than how they sound. Words are tactile. I feel like I can hold them in my hands and throw them at people; I feel like I might scratch myself on their edges; they roll around in my mouth like barbed marbles. I shove and bend and crank words to form images and rhythms that I hope snag the reader's attention.

This tactility stems from two things: my reliance on my other senses and my experience with closed captioning and subtitles. I process the world visually and kinetically, so I look for action and movement rather than listen for cues. I look for depth and space. When I read and write, words begin as two dimensional, and then they begin to acquire shadows; if it's going well, they eventually begin to somersault across the page, and by the end of the story or poem or book the words have been imprinted on me, and I end up acquiring a sort of textual muscle memory, the sort of memory that allows athletes to easily slide into a routine whenever they step onto a deadlift platform or perform a long jump. As I write, I try to translate that kinetic aspect by using muscular, concrete language.

In my poetry collection *Beautiful Mutants*, I included a sequence called "Deaf Speech," a hodgepodge of prose poems, neologisms, alphabetical forms, gibberish, and conversations with Stephen Dedalus. With the glee of a child watching two scorpions wrestle, I test the limits of language by fucking shit up—that is, both by disrupting the structures of English and by embracing my inability to hear properly. The alphabetical forms, poems of twenty-six lines with each line dedicated to one specific letter, convey the restrictive, oppressive aspects of English: "An awkward aria / begins, blurred, bumbling, / causing crippling cacophony, / delivering discursive detritus." The prose parts, particularly the conversations, extol the linguistic freedom that comes with deafness; deafness frees one from the rules of language. The Ukrainian-born Russian-Jewish-American poet Ilya Kaminsky, also deaf, calls this phenomenon "wreckage": "My syntax is wrecked enough already.... My English is the world I make as I go. It is already a private language, an imaginary language." If James Joyce were alive today, he'd probably be learning every Sign Language he could get his hands on. As my speaker talks to Mr. Dedalus, deafness becomes a city made of language in which walls are elastic and letters have sex and reproduce words. As the speaker says, "you cannot be trapped by language if you can't hear it properly." I also assert that deaf accents form part of the world's tapestry of accents. My voice is accented, and when I meet people for the first time they often ask if I'm from Ireland or Australia. Usually I tell them I'm deaf, but sometimes I don't. Sometimes, as I write in one of the prose sections, "I just speak and people believe me when I say oh yes I love Sydney." My deaf speech helps me pretend to be other people, to slide in and out of other accents.

Although sound does occasionally dictate what I write, it's impossible for me to separate sound and feeling. I say *feeling* in every sense of the word: the emotions attached to sounds, the tactile sensations sounds give off, the instincts sounds can trigger. When I talk, I feel as though I'm pulling the membranous strings of a meaty violin. This mixture of sound and feeling makes it difficult for me to write sonnets, villanelles, and other rhyming forms. Whenever I attempt rhymes, I feel that I'm picking up Lego blocks and slotting them into what I hope are the right places. My rhymes feel laboured, concocted. They don't follow natural speech the way hearing writers' sonnets do. The one sonnet I feel semi-confident about appears in *Beautiful Mutants*:

> I can ignore you and get away with it.
> If I turn my eyes away from you your words
> fall uselessly around me. I like it,
> actually, turning away towards
> more idle, empty spaces and meeting
> the images I find there: dense constraints
> that thicken the air, anxious glances of fleeting
> whimsy, how people toss themselves against
> each other. I like how, when I turn away,
> I see everything: duplicitous faces,
> illusory colours, and ignored graces.
> Honestly, I prefer to live this way,
> with an excuse to ignore you, and
> just enough hearing to know the difference.

The rhyme, the rhythm, the meter—they're all off, which of course is the point, since the sonnet concludes a sequence called "Hearing Test." Part of becoming comfortable as a writer has meant becoming comfortable as a deaf person and employing the unique rhythms that plod and rumble and titter in my head and heart. I doubt I'll ever write a perfect sonnet, but then I'm not sure I want to.

Other deaf poets combine sound with action rather than feeling, as in this passage from Ilya Kaminsky's "9AM Bombardment":

> It has begun: they climb the trolleys
> at the thief market, breaking
> all their moments in half. And the army officers

in the clanging trolleys shoot at our neighbors' faces
and in their ears. And the army officer says: Boys!
    Girls!
take your partner two steps. Shoot.

Here, physical actions—climbing, breaking, shooting,
running give the lines a forceful, percussive rhythm
that quickly generates momentum. We can see the
army officers' stomps, their brusque gestures.

Kaminsky also uses repetition in his poems, but
his repetition has a different purpose than, say, the
refrains in Dylan Thomas's "Do Not Go Gentle into
That Good Night," as illustrated in the last stanza of
"9AM Bombardment":

It has begun: I saw how the blue canary of my country
picks breadcrumbs from each soldier's hair
picks breadcrumbs from each soldier's eyes.
Rain leaves the earth and falls straight up as it should.
To have a country, so important,
to run into walls, into streetlights, into loved ones,
    as one should.
Watch their legs as they run and fall.
I have seen the blue canary of my country
watch their legs as they run and fall.

Rather than simply repeating phrases as musical
refrains to emphasize a message, Kaminsky's speaker
repeats phrases as though to be reassured in the face of
horrific circumstances, as though the ability to articulate might slip away. According to Kaminsky, the
poem is part of a "story of a pregnant woman and her
husband living during an epidemic of deafness and
civil unrest . . . in Eastern Europe." But the ability to

articulate doesn't slip away—not as long as the speaker continues to use it, and Kaminsky takes full advantage of his unique relationship with language.

My own propensity for embracing difference and employing tactile language shows through even more in my novel *Mantis Dreams: The Journal of Dr. Dexter Ripley*. Dexter has Charcot-Marie-Tooth disease and processes the world through his disability. To him, disability is more than a physical, mental, or intellectual condition; it's a philosophy, a way of seeing the world. Rather than create a disabled character who feels sorry for himself—as I learned through my academic research, there are way too many of them—I wanted a rambunctious asshole who generates headlong narrative momentum by outraging those around him and promoting his philosophy. Dexter writes,

> I want my ideas to work. I want them to flood some previously untouched rind in people's brains with a charged, awakening crackle, as though they've been slammed with gospel. I want canes and crutches to be raised like M16s. I want wheelchair users to roll like tanks into crowded rooms. I want tongues as loose and jittery as mine to hop around the earth like fish suddenly turned amphibious, hollering instead of gasping, chanting instead of croaking. I want the growls and grunts and yips and huffs and shouts and warbles of all my floppy-mouthed comrades to be taken as calls to arms, as wondrous philosophy, as the voices of our times.

For Dexter, an idea is more than an abstract thought—it is a physical experience. Same with the pain he feels: his disease causes high arches in his feet and scoliosis in his spine, and I try to capture these symptoms in his propulsive, sardonic voice.

• • •

Although I hated getting my hearing aids when I was six, my parents bought a different gadget that I loved immediately. I remember walking into the living room one day to find my dad hooking a small black box up to the television.

I tapped his shoulder. "What's that?"

"It's a captioning machine," he said.

"What's a cashpinning machine?"

"Captioning, captioning machine. It's for you. When you watch hockey or *Ghostbusters*, you can see the words at the bottom of the screen. Here, let's try it. Pick a movie."

He moved aside while I rummaged through our VHS collection. I picked up *Clash of the Titans* and put it into the VCR. Dad turned on the TV and pushed a button on the captioning machine; a small green light blinked on. We both sat on the floor and watched. Like a small black scroll, the words unrolled across the screen as Perseus and his mother were thrown into a coffin and cast away to the sea. Dad and I grinned at each other.

"What do you think?" he said.

I nodded, in awe of the device.

I was proud to discover I didn't miss too many sounds. The captioning filled small gaps and showed me what was beyond my hearing: rustles, trills, screeches, shrieks. Prior to receiving the captioning box, dialogue sounded like mumbling, with a clear word here and there; now I could confirm what I was hearing.

There were other benefits too: not only was I learning to read while watching television, but also I found a way around parental censorship. My parents could mute the television, but they couldn't mute the captioning at the same time, so while I didn't hear the words *fuck* or *shit* or *asshole* I sure as hell saw them.

Although reading poems, novels, and short stories has helped me learn literary conventions, years of watching television shows and films with captioning and subtitles has had a tremendous impact on the way I write—not to mention helping me ace just about every spelling test from Grade Two onward. The rhythm of captioning, the way the words appear on the screen, the number of words that appear at once—all of these aspects affect how I experience language, which in turn influences how I conceive and execute my work, especially poetry. Over the years, I've noticed my line breaks in poetry tend to end naturally at roughly the same point, about three-quarters of the way across the page, much like a full line of captioning. The first two poems in *Beautiful Mutants*, "The Spider" and "View from a Saskatchewan Country Hospital Room," show the poetic effect of captioning. Pentameter and dimeter and hexameter mean zilch—the unrolling rhythm of black-and-white words governs my line lengths. Captioning is full of enjambments; it makes a great film or television speech into a poem. When I try to write shorter lines, as with some of the pieces in the sequence "The Alberta Provincial Training School for Mental Defectives," it feels forced, unnatural.

• • •

Every language is foreign to me. The factory in my head lacks the standard machinery that most people possess. Most people have a built-in language processing centre, a standard-issue droid; mine is C-3PO, built from scratch using salvaged and worn equipment. The result: I'm hyperaware of which words I use.

I'm well versed in gibberish. Every day I walk around my house saying things like "Smeffity perfidy wankity bleh!" and "Bastarding farkus!" If my wife's around, I might say something like "Naaah I nay nassemen biffery negaty peppers!" (Translation: "I don't want peppers, my dear. Love you.")

I'm well versed in gibberish because I'm afraid of words. I'm afraid of misusing them. I'm afraid of mispronouncing them. I'm afraid of appearing ignorant or inadequate. Because I'm a writer, people expect me to have the English language in a half-nelson. They think I can make the language cry "Uncle!" and easily find the right words and deliver them in precisely the right order. But I can't, at least not right away. When I write, I sometimes feel like I'm rooting around in an alien's slimy nest and pulling out pods and sticking them into an incubator. Finding the right words takes time, whether I'm speaking or writing. I need to trust the words I use. Words are deceptive little fucks. I'll read a word like *collegiate* and later use it in writing, but if I've never heard it said aloud I'll wonder if a character is using it right, and I'll look up synonyms to ensure I'm using it in the right context. Then later I'll use the word in conversation, and someone will tell me I'm saying it wrong.

"Collee-git?"

"No, eejit. Collee-jit."

Whenever I sit down to write, or to talk with a friend, that anxiety is always there.

Because of my deafness, conversations and meetings have to be structured a certain way. I prefer one-on-one meetings so I can concentrate on the person's face, and I avoid busy, noisy places as a general rule. People have to look at me when they speak; otherwise, their words sound like mumbling, and I tune them out and retreat into my imagination—not necessarily a bad thing, especially if the conversation's boring, but if the conversation's interesting, or if I'm looking to build a friendship, I need to understand what's being said.

On top of the anxiety I carry into every interaction—will I understand them?—I carry another: how does having such structured conversations affect my ability to write realistic dialogue? How can I develop an ear for engaging banter when most of the conversations I have are rigidly structured? Conversations are lively things. People talk out of turn. The subject changes quickly. There are often important or revealing subtexts. Conversations are usually governed by spontaneity, and how can I convey that spontaneity on the page if I seldom experience it in real life?

Imagination, of course. I don't hear everything, but I hear some things, and my imagination fills in the gaps. My deafness has helped my imagination develop: if I'm interested in a conversation, I can keep up with it by taking little snippets I hear and reconstructing the context in my head; if I'm not interested in it, I'll do as my sonnet suggests and turn toward other people and imagine the dialogue they're having. Most people do this anyway, but being deaf makes boring people easier to ignore.

I have a strong suspicion that authors who regularly engage in lively, witty, or antagonistic conversations in real life are more likely to write strong dialogue.

Mordecai Richler frequently engaged in—and started—vigorous arguments, and his novels appear to show the fruits of his provocative nature. In novel after novel, from *The Apprenticeship of Duddy Kravitz* to *Barney's Version*, Richler shows his gift for banter. Brad Fraser is another writer with a history of provocation. His plays *Unidentified Human Remains and the True Nature of Love*, *Poor Super Man*, and *Kill Me Now* are stuffed with dazzling dialogue. If most of what you hear is boring shit, then the conversations you write might bore you in turn, and you'll lose your reader's attention.

While I was preparing my play *Ultrasound* for production, most of the rewrites I did focused on making conversations more realistic. In the play's first scene, Alphonse, a Deaf man, tries to avoid talking about having a child; then he tries to delay the subject; then he tries to convince Miranda, his wife, that they're not ready, that a child is too expensive. Miranda demands they talk about it right then, forcing Alphonse to admit his real hesitation: he's worried they'll have a hearing child. He wants their child to be deaf, and because of past abuse by his hearing uncle he will not tolerate a hearing child in his household.

My initial draft of the play revealed Alphonse's hesitation way too quickly. I'm an impatient person, and I have a tendency to want to get to the meaty parts right away; as a result, my first drafts lack suspense. Because of my deafness, I didn't have as strong an understanding of conversations as I thought. I spend much of my time alone and in my head, so I don't have many in-person discussions, let alone discussions that escalate into conflicts. Working with the actors and the director proved to be crucial to developing that ability to write better dialogue.

Captioning and subtitles help me in this regard too. They provide a visual guide to the rhythms and tics of how people speak: which words they use, how they use them, and when they use them. When I reread *Mantis Dreams* or *The Bus*, I see the influence of captioning in the dialogue; there's a subtle skidding rhythm. Captioning can also have a detrimental effect in that my characters' voices might all sound the same. I work hard to give my characters individual voices so they don't appear to be coming from the same place. I want them to speak and act as though they're unique, organic beings with their own backgrounds, people you could run into in the street and gab with over coffee. Few writers are able to grant each of their characters a unique voice. William Faulkner is one; Toni Morrison is another; Annie Proulx can do it too. It seems the influence of captioning, in which all characters' words look the same, hinders as well as helps.

• • •

I have to be careful with my words, not only because I write about disability, deafness, abortion, euthanasia, and eugenics, and not only because I take my job as a writer seriously, but also because I am a human being who wishes the best for everyone and works hard to understand the perspectives of others. Part of the work of empathy means using appropriate language. In our contemporary world of continuous information sharing, there is no longer any excuse for getting things wrong, whether it is a word choice or a character decision or a plot point that demonstrates prejudice toward others. We can no longer say that books are just books and films are just films and albums are just albums and

paintings are just paintings that exist completely outside politics. Any act of creation carries with it the circumstances of that creation: who's in power, what the
artist is worried about, which other cultural texts are
being produced. Writers—that is, real writers, not privileged wonks—are willing to reduce their own egos in
the service of the work. They will do whatever makes
the work better and more authentic. Such writers work
hard to understand the pains and joys of others and
build from that knowledge to try to create something
organic and beautiful that helps diminish the pain. Our
artistic landscape sees enough privilege. It's too easy to
write something misogynistic or racist or ableist and
then simply call it a character quality. There must be a
reckoning; it must be thoroughly addressed.

I am deaf, but as a straight white cis man I occupy
a privileged position. I've made many mistakes in my
own work. I've had characters use harmful language
without properly working through that language, and
I'm working to be better so I can carefully differen-
tiate between discriminatory language and language
that criticizes or satirizes that discrimination while
at the same time reclaiming those harmful terms or
suggesting alternatives. Because that is a writer's role:
to provide words when old or harmful words no longer
work. In *Mantis Dreams*, Dexter uses the word *cripple*
not to be an ableist asshole but to take back the word
from able-bodied people by diminishing its prejudicial
weight and rechristening it as a term of pride. Dexter
also comes up with a new word for disability, *Dexterity*,
though the word is as much about his ego as it is about
making disability into a positive quality.

I'm afraid of words, but that's a good thing, a healthy
thing. I hope I will always be afraid of words, handling

them the way an immunologist handles test tubes gurgling with viruses, because that fear makes me aware of their impacts, and that awareness is crucial for creating a truly accessible and welcoming world.

ON VOICE

Everyone has two voices, a speaking voice and an interior voice. Some people speak through their mouths, some through their hands; others speak through their bellies and elbows and feet, or through balloons and pipe cleaners, but everyone has two voices.

These two voices often influence each other, and for writers their interior voices are their strongest ones. Much of my anxiety as a writer blooms from the tension between my speaking voice and my interior voice. My speaking voice is accented, and even though I've had speech therapy I have difficulty pronouncing certain words. I stumble when I say "February" or "professorial" or any other word loaded with r's (which sucks, because I was born in February). Because most of us are taught to sound out words when we learn to read, our interior voices grow out of our speaking voices, so when we read we hear a voice in our heads. If while we read we come across a word we don't know how to say out loud, our interior voices trip and stumble, and we have to take time to sound out the word, and if we continually come across words like that we lose interest in what we're reading.

A hearing writer's speaking and interior voices appear to have a close, even symbiotic, relationship. One continually feeds off the other. Writers with great ears for rhythm and dialogue, such as Richard Van Camp, Lynn Coady, John Irving, Hunter S. Thompson, and Eden Robinson, appear to possess the literary equivalent of perfect pitch. They seem to have fostered and honed the relationship between their speaking and interior voices until they are almost indistinguishable.

Van Camp is a particularly good example. He is as skilled an oral storyteller as he is a writer. In his novel *The Lesser Blessed*, his sentences pulse with rhythm. His narrator, Larry Sole, tells the story with a grim yet bolstering musicality. Music is a crucial undercurrent of Larry's narration. It's not just his allusions to The Cure or Iron Maiden or Fields of the Nephilim; the sentences themselves can be sung—indeed, they are meant to be sung in the guttural, wailing voice of a moshing teenager: "There was the terrible stuck of Bubblicious gum in my hair, the chocolate stain of Jazz's blood on my fist. There was a rash on my face where I had shaved, and the words 'I'm a boxer' bounced around my twisted skull." In the novel's acknowledgements, Van Camp states that "the writing here was inspired by the music and talent" of more than a dozen bands. His writing has a rhythm dictated by the sounds of words rather than their feel or appearance; as a result, his writing sounds natural in our heads.

For deaf writers, the relationship between speaking and interior voices yields a variety of results. Sign Language performers such as Dawn Jani Birley and Ian Sanborn have externalized their interiority, lending their compositions a raw immediacy that few textual writers can achieve. In their openness, grace, and symbolism, Sign Languages are perhaps the most sensual and poetic languages in the world. To that end, Joanne Weber's writing exhibits beautiful, sensual density. Weber is fluent in both English and American Sign Language, and in her poetry book *The Pear Orchard* and her memoir *The Deaf House* her lines and sentences have a physical heft to them that reveals a dynamic relationship between her speaking and interior voices. In his written poetry,

Bruce Hunter appears to write from a place of pure interiority, as in "The Scale" in *Two O'Clock Creek: Poems
New and Selected*:

> Dawn's lightning in the treetops
> charged with nitrogen.
> Air punky with electricity.
> The crown of an old chestnut split.
>
> Lifted into the damage,
> angel of mercy in a hardhat.
> Distant thunder, wind enough
> to make this a warning of worse.

Although his lines are short, they are thick with contemplation. Thanks to their assertive description,
Hunter's poems have a gutsy, Studs Terkel–like tempo
that demands attention.

The relationship between my speaking and interior
voices is more dysfunctional than symbiotic. I can't
verbalize a story worth shit; I always have to go back
and insert crucial details. If I can't pronounce a word
out loud, I usually won't use it in my writing, which
wouldn't bother me except my deaf accent limits which
words I can pronounce. At the same time, I've noticed
a curious development over the past few years: my
interior voice has become bolder and more articulate
than my speaking voice. My interior voice has begun
to detach itself from my speaking voice and become its
own unique being. I like to think it's a sign I'm becoming
more comfortable as a writer, but it's more likely because
I've been losing more of my hearing, which has affected
my speech, so my interior voice has evolved in response
to the degeneration of my speaking voice. The latter is

slowly failing, a muscle being drained of its strength, whereas my interior voice is an effervescent black-and-purple organ that lives just to the right of my heart, a pulsing, grumbling, endocrinal vessel of love, despair, empathy, gratitude, and giddy absurdity. Everything I think and feel flushes through this organ with skidding peristaltic rhythms, and since I began writing about deafness and disability the organ's walls have become stronger, and its output has become clearer.

ON SILENCE

We live in a noisy world. Noise bombards us: washers, dryers, motorcycles, lawn mowers, stereos, photocopiers, fax machines, dogs, cats, birds, bats, cows, coyotes, oven timers, microwaves, PA systems, fluorescent lights, televisions, computers, video games, cell phones, jacked-up trucks, souped-up cars, along with all the little in-between sounds, such as scratching, scraping, rustling, ripping, sliding, slamming, bubbling, splashing, knocking, smacking, chopping, slicing, creaking, crunching, cranking, crinkling, crumpling, whipping, flicking, whooshing, whiffing, whistling, hissing, and swishing. Not to mention fucking people.

Whenever I think about noise, I imagine it surrounding me like a wall of ghosts. I can't hear all of it, so I process it in visual terms and create an image to help me understand it. Some noises even have colours: my wife's voice has a soft creamy hue, coinciding with her skin; truck engines present as a chugging, puffing grey, like an octogenarian smoking hashish; heavy metal crashes and jangles in sharp black-and-red lines, like the stock graph for a failing company.

With all of the noise in the world, it seems to be a miracle most of us aren't deaf. I often read about how more and more people are losing their hearing because of the increasing level of noise. My deafness has helped me see the value of noise and the lack thereof. It makes me question what is really worth listening to. What music do we prefer to hear? Which voices do we cherish the most? Which sounds do we miss when we retire, or move, or lose our hearing? What do we really need to hear?

My deafness has also shown me the preciousness of silence. Many people are suspicious of silence. We often read silence as indicating that something is wrong or that something terrible is about to happen. Silence discomforts people. We don't like to be alone with our thoughts, so we try to fill that silence as much as possible by fiddling with our phones or twirling fidget spinners. We never just stand and observe; if we do, people question us and, on occasion, call the police.

My deafness prompts me to look for what's missing in a particular situation, and in our noisy world we're missing silence. Silence is among the most beautiful things in the world, not only because it's so precious. Even if you have just a few seconds of silence at work, or in the car, or at home, that brief, brief silence has a sacredness to it, a quality we immediately appreciate, because it allows you to hear yourself, and when you can hear yourself you can begin to think, and imagine, and grow. If there's one thing I appreciate about my deafness more than anything else, it's that enhanced ability to hear myself think. My interior voice has become much more articulate and forceful than my speaking voice, and that enhanced development has bolstered my evolution as a writer. So, if I have any advice to give, it would be "Sshhh."

Although deafness and silence are related, deafness is not necessarily synonymous with silence. It is not simply a condition of non-hearing; it can be a condition of hearing things differently. Many hearing people believe one is either fully deaf or fully hearing. They seem amazed whenever I speak, saying things like, "Wow, I didn't know deaf people could speak, and you speak very well." They say these things in the same tone as when they congratulate their dogs for rolling over. When they say these things, I have to resist the urge to reply, "Thank you, you supercalifragilisticexpialidouche bag."

Silence does not necessarily mean nothingness either. Silence carries many meanings. It signifies peace and safety, the quiet of armistice. It is the lack of a voice and the trace of a voice. It unsettles and discomforts us. It suggests death. It suggests contemplation. It is often interpreted as indicating complicity or agreement, especially in dictatorial regimes. It is a method of rebellion, of refusing to testify against or speak in favour of those in power. It can function as a shield and as a weapon. It can imply guilt and innocence. It enfolds us when we pray and worship. It surrounds us when we create.

For me as a writer, silence is both an ally and an enemy. On the page, it is both the space between words and a way of speaking. Silence can speak more profoundly than any word. Sometimes the things we want to say the most can't (and shouldn't) be shaped into words.

In my poem "Hearing Test," the speaker describes listening to the audiologist read a list of words to test the range of his hearing:

She says, Say the word Ate.	Ape.
Say the word Gave.	Dave.
Say the word Rip.	Writ.
Say the word Up.	Ut.

The gap of white space signifies the speaker's deafness; the audiologist's words only partially cross the gulf of silence. I slam the speaker's responses against the margin of the page, suggesting the marginalization of the deaf in a hearing world.

Poets appear to be more adept than fiction writers at employing silence, specifically the silence of implicitness. "Tell it slant" and "tell it silent" are, to me, interchangeable. Poetry is thought to be so difficult not because of the words themselves but because of the silence surrounding them. It's a silence that tickles our chins, a silence that dares us. We always ask "What does it mean?" and are met with silence. A symbol can't function properly without the silence that protects it; a metaphor's thrust stems from silence. If everything was explicit, we wouldn't read Yeats or Tennyson or Dickinson or Plath or Angelou or Browning or Thomas or any of the poets whose work has formed the foundation of English literature. Although Plath's "Daddy" and Thomas's "Do Not Go Gentle into That Good Night" appear to say all they need to say, both carry heavy undercurrents of silence. When we read these poems, we think the poets have so much more to say. In her poem, Plath compares her father to Hitler and her husband to a vampire, and she ends with the devastating line "Daddy, daddy, you bastard, I'm through." But she is never through. She can never say enough: her emotions are an enormous snarl that mere words cannot clarify. Thomas, meanwhile, expresses his despair in the face of his father's death. His love for his father is clear, yet the word *love* never arises.

In these poems and in thousands of others, there is as much unspoken as there is spoken, as many gaps between verses as there are verses themselves, saying to the reader "Stop here. Think for a moment. Absorb." A finished poem represents a poet's best attempt at employing and articulating a specific silence. Silence is as much the bedrock of poetry as words themselves.

• • •

I grew up watching horror movies. I love them all: *Halloween, The Texas Chain Saw Massacre, The Wicker Man, The Exorcist, The Omen, Rosemary's Baby, Friday the 13th, Child's Play.* I love the stories, the blood, the camp, the psychological triggers, the suspense, and, most of all, the silence. Horror employs silence more often and more effectively than most other film genres. Whenever silence arises, it triggers our imaginations: "Where is he? Was that a noise? Dammit, where is he?!" We have no choice but to give ourselves up to the silence, which conceals the killers and is often embodied in the killers themselves. Michael Myers, Jason Voorhees, Leatherface—silent killers all. They have no use for words. They speak solely through their actions. Silence is their strength. If they were to speak, they wouldn't be anywhere near as terrifying.

When used properly, whether it's in unspoken dialogue, a concealed detail, or an indeterminate ending, silence can be an effective storytelling tool. Words sometimes get in the way of a story; they belabour the point. Although there's something to be said for writers who fill every possible space with words—writers such as Leo Tolstoy and Marcel Proust and George Eliot and Joyce Carol Oates and David Foster Wallace, who seek to present as complete a portrait of a time, place, and/ or person as possible—such writers tend to overwrite and do the work for the reader. On the page, as in life, we shouldn't feel obligated to fill every possible space with words.

Just as the best horror movie directors understand the intrinsic value of silence, so too do the best writers; Cormac McCarthy is one such writer. His novel *The Road* employs silence in a profoundly pervasive manner. In this novel, America has been hit by an unknown apocalyptic event. The world is cold and grey; ashen snow falls. Almost everyone is dead. A man and his son travel alone, scrounging for food as they try to survive long enough to make it to the coast. Although most post-apocalyptic stories relish detailing exactly what brought about the end of the world, *The Road* doesn't. The best writers know when to let the reader do the work—when to keep silent, in other words—and McCarthy makes exquisite use of silence. We've already experienced so many possibilities in other stories— nuclear war, chemical warfare, disease, famine, natural disaster, alien invasion—that we don't need to know what happened. We can fill in the blanks ourselves, and when we do we become more invested in the story.

• • •

I don't know how anyone can be a writer without becoming comfortable with silence. How can you lis- ten to your interior voice with other voices and noises clattering all around you? How can you observe while texting a friend and listening to Lady Gaga on your headphones? Even though I'm deaf, I require total quiet when I write. I shut the door to my office and let my wife know I'm working so she doesn't disturb me. It seems that, in addition to reading and writing as often as possible, developing writers need to learn to deafen themselves, to learn to live inside silence. In *On Writing: A Memoir of the Craft*, Stephen King talks about "creative sleep," stating that writers must learn to dream while they're awake. We can't sleep without silence, and we can't dream without it either. We already deafen ourselves when we read; it's simply a matter of extending that silence into the writing room, of creating a shelter around ourselves so we're free to dream.

• • •

Every time I sit down to write, I work to hunker down into my bivouac of comforting silence while at the same time fending off another, more malicious silence.

This latter silence pervades my chosen subject matter. Deafness and disability upset people. We don't like to discuss them because the subject exposes our ignorance. Many of us lack the vocabulary because we have little or no interaction with Deaf and disabled people. They are often ignored, and if not ignored they are mocked, harassed, beaten, institutionalized, and even killed. Authors are afraid to write about them because it's taboo, or because they think it's politically incorrect, or because their empathy becomes frayed and then ends. They don't want to occupy that imaginative headspace and see themselves as deaf, or as paraplegic, or as someone with Down syndrome.

As disability scholars such as Sally Chivers have pointed out, we in Canada appear to have two governing narratives with regard to disability: the Terry Fox narrative, which focuses on those who overcome obstacles and succeed despite their disabilities, and the Tracy Latimer narrative, which portrays disabled people as tragic figures to be pitied. If a story about disability doesn't suit either narrative, Canadians don't want to hear it. For disabled people to be heard, they must be either a hero or dead. These narratives impose an oppressive silence on Deaf and disabled people, and within that oppressive silence they experience systemic abuse, neglect, segregation, and dehumanization. As Elie Wiesel reminds us in his Nobel Peace Prize acceptance speech, "silence encourages the tormentor, never the tormented." As a result, one of my chief motivations as a writer is to exorcise that restrictive silence, to blast these subjects open using new, refreshing language that allows us to talk candidly about them. It's a slightly ironic proposition: from within my carefully cultivated silence, I seek to extinguish another silence. The former is driven by empathy, a yearning to reach out and discover the souls of others; the latter is hateful and seeks to eradicate and bury those souls.

My poem "Asymmetry" tells the story of a teenage amputee named Zach. His leg has been cut off, and he sees it as a point of pride—and sexiness. In the poem's first section, he photographs himself naked, then posts his picture on a dating website for amputees; in a later section, he attends a sexual health clinic and takes pride in the warts that crowd his cock: "He thought of how he'd be seen: a fifteen year old amputee / swinging his way into the clinic with a toothy grin and red cheeks." He indulges in the "melody of fetishes" he discovers:

> acrotomophilia, apotemnophilia—those who fuck
>   amputees
> and those who want to be fucked as amputees.
> Last week he was online and chatted with a woman
> who'd had her hand cut off by a lawnmower
> and declared she'd never use a vibrator again.

I wanted these images to shock the reader—not simply because they're x-rated, but also because many readers have never imagined amputees having dirty sex. I wanted to dive into the subject lustily, greedily, matching Zach's sex drive and his need for connection. Deaf and disabled people continue to be abused, segregated, and killed because we don't talk about these things. By suggesting that amputees can be just as filthy as the rest of us, I'm not only subverting the reader's expectations—that is, the oppressive silence of normalcy—but also showing what's possible when we accept this fact.

But writing alone does not help alleviate oppressive silence. Although Deaf and disabled writers such as Ryan Knighton, Bruce Hunter, David Freeman, Joanne Weber, Lynx Sainte-Marie, Jane Eaton Hamilton, Dorothy Ellen Palmer, Leah Lakshmi Piepzna-Samarasinha, Debbie Patterson, Kim Clark, Paul Power, and Alan Shain have begun to whittle down that silence, they can't do it by themselves. Literature relies as much on—if not more on—relationships than on books and poems and articles. It can't exist without publishers and readers; unfortunately, Deaf and disabled writers have had tremendous difficulty trying to present their work to the public because publishers and readers prefer stereotypical stories that perpetuate the aforementioned familiar narratives. Few Canadians, on their own initiative, will pick up a book about amputees having filthy sex, or men with cerebral palsy hollering and cavorting in a men's bathroom, or a deaf woman selling heroin. Canadians prefer Deaf and disabled people to be safely tucked in the wings, away from their attention. It's troubling that, in a nation that prides itself on diversity, Deaf and disabled people can't be heard, so the responsibility of breaking down that silence lies not only with writers but also with publishers and the readers they serve.

ON OBSERVING

In June 2015, my wife, Debbie, and I flew to London for a short vacation. We saw a lot of the usual stuff: Westminster Abbey, London Bridge, Parliament, Buckingham Palace, Dickens's house. One day we went to the Courtauld Gallery, a beautiful gallery that houses numerous major works, including paintings by Degas, Van Gogh, Monet, and Bruegel. We worked our way through the gallery, admiring the architecture as much as the artworks themselves. Ahead of us was a group of twentysomethings who stopped in front of each painting, took pictures with their phones, then moved on. They never studied a painting for more than ten seconds. I imagined their brains as pages written on with invisible ink.

Deb and I were about three-quarters of the way through the gallery when we came to a painting by Chaim Soutine, a twentieth-century Parisian painter. The painting, *Young Woman in a White Blouse*, depicted a woman with black hair and a warped face. The description read "This painting is typical of [Soutine's] approach to the figure, which he distorts expressively to convey a heightened sense of emotional and psychological tension." Deb and I spent a few minutes studying the painting before moving on to a pair of Degases.

She started gushing about a Van Gogh she'd seen earlier, and I, having heard her gush about Van Gogh numerous times before, tuned out and looked back at the Soutine painting. A young woman stood before it. A long rip zagged down her coat sleeve. Her canvas skater shoes were old and frayed; the toe of her right shoe flapped up like a puppet. Her eyes were clenched blue coils. She stared at the painting and panted once and bit her lip, as though the woman in the frame was her dead lover. She leaned forward, slowly pushing out her jaw. She seemed to want to be absorbed into the painting, and I had the feeling she'd come to the gallery for this painting alone. She never noticed me watching her. I found myself making up a story about her and the painting: she and her lover used to come to this gallery and look at the painting, and they would joke that her lover looked like Soutine's subject; then, when her lover died, the young woman had a dream that her lover's soul found a home in the painting, and she'd been visiting the gallery every day since.

"Adam? Are you coming?"

I turned and followed Deb into the next room, where the twentysomethings were already leaving. I glanced back at the young woman, whose coiled blue eyes remained fastened on the painting.

My deafness allows me to withdraw from whatever social context I'm in and observe what else is going on around me. In doing so, I notice things other people don't. Sometimes I notice anomalies: a frayed power cord, a nervous tic, a hair floating on the air, a dog's empty water dish, a broken window. Sometimes I notice gaps: books left out of a series, ingredients missing from a recipe, songs dropped from a band's concert set. Sometimes I notice people, such as the young woman in the gallery, people to whom others pay little or no attention, people who aren't seen or heard, people who, like me, have built shelters around themselves to distance themselves from the dense, simmering stew of humanity.

All writers incorporate their observations into their writing. What separate us are the details we notice.

Some writers have enormous radars for details—nothing escapes their attention. Tom Wolfe's writing is stuffed with details: the music clattering through the speakers, the posters peeling off the telephone poles, the hairstyles of his denizens, the accents and tones and timbres of motley voices, the smells of pot and booze and paint and sweat, the headlines of the day. Part of the appeal of *The Electric Kool-Aid Acid Test* lies in Wolfe's ability to replicate the sensory experience of the 1960s:

> Suddenly he is like a ping-pong ball in a flood of sensory stimuli, heart beating, blood coursing, breath suspiring, teeth grating, hand moving over the percale sheet over those thousands of minute warfy woofings like a brush fire, sun glow and the highlight on a stainless-steel rod, quite a little movie you have going on in that highlight there, Hondo, Technicolors, pick each one out like fishing for neon gumballs with a steam shovel in the Funtime Arcade. . . .

Wolfe assaults our senses, presenting the 1960s in prose that reads like a Merry Prankster babbling and chanting from within the synaesthesiac whorl of an acid trip.

Other writers have more focused radars. Ryan Knighton's book *Cockeyed* not only offers a hilarious and imaginative exploration of blindness but also conveys the impact of blindness on language. Every word is dialed toward conveying the experience of blindness. Just as my writing has grown out of my deafness, so too has Knighton's writing grown out of his blindness, and his observations of growing up with retinitis pigmentosa and learning to navigate the world with a white cane are both provocative and exhilarating.

I sometimes worry that my writing is too focused, that I'm writing within a vacuum, that what I've seen and experienced of the world are too narrow, that few people can relate to what I'm trying to say. But then I read writers such as Emily Dickinson and William Blake and Thomas Pynchon and Allen Ginsberg, whose works are crammed with cryptic symbols and esoterica. It's not the writer's job to pander to the reader; the writer challenges the reader. Readers must attempt to decode whatever observations writers present— must give themselves up, in other words, and occupy a writer's unique headspace and experience the world the way the writer does.

ON STEREOTYPES

Imagine your neighbourhood grocery store. Smell the linoleum, the vegetables, the freshly packaged meat, the spilled milk in the dairy section. See the dreary yellow sales advertisements as you wander through the aisles. See the range of cereals, the different types of mustard, the various brands of frozen pizza. You know them all. You've been here so many times.

Similar to your neighbourhood grocery store is a store where writers shop, except instead of mayonnaise or Frosted Flakes they buy characters. This is the Store of Stereotypes. Thousands of writers visit this store every day. Each of its products is wrapped in cellophane and ready for immediate use: the Antisocial Scientist, the Cripple Who Wants to Die, the Drunk Indigenous Man, the Jewish Guy Whose Mom Dotes over Him, the Street-Smart Black Kid, the Deaf Boy Who Misunderstands Everything, the Girl Who Seems Ugly but Improves Instantly When Her Glasses Are Removed, the Butch Lesbian.

Most writers shop at this store. It costs them a simple pittance, a few measly synaptic sparks for characters they've seen and used dozens of times before. They don't put in the time and effort to save up their synaptic sparks and spend them on truly original characters, those who do things differently, those who seem like real people instead of characters. We know these writers as well as we know our favourite cereal brands. These writers tell the same stories over and over. They soothe us rather than provoke us.

Being different often prompts writers to examine their preconceptions about people and about themselves and to avoid stereotypes. In an article in *Open Book*, Jen Sookfong Lee describes just how oppressive literary expectations can be when writing about Asian women:

> There is a kind of comfort with novels like *The Joy Luck Club* and *The End of East*. The oppression almost always comes in the form of systemic oppression, of a government or war that hurts or marginalizes people, and not at the hands of individuals we can recognize. They are set in the past and contemporary readers can shake their heads at how bad things used to be, without reflecting too hard on how bad things still are right now.

After discovering how oppressive literary expectations were, and how they had manifested within her own work, Lee decided to break away from those expectations and craft a different kind of novel, the excellent *The Conjoined*.

Thanks to my deafness, I've been able to avoid the Store of Stereotypes, especially when it comes to Deaf and disabled characters. I'm suspicious of convention the way a diligent shopper is suspicious of the ingredients in canned ham. My deafness prompts me to go in different directions, to use fresh phrasing, to experiment with forms, to feature people from whom we seldom hear. To that end, I've created my own little pasture for my poems and stories to graze. The pasture might not be big, and it might take more time for my stories to develop, but by the time they're ready they're sturdy, well fed, and prepared for whatever grinder I might put them through.

In my chapbook *Bereft*, I wrote a short poem about the Nazis' euthanasia program, and though it told a compelling story I thought it was incomplete. I sought more information: books, articles, websites, personal testimonies. There are many stories of Jewish and Polish and Romanian people surviving the concentration camps, but I couldn't find any stories about disabled people surviving the euthanasia centres.

I had to write more about it. I had to find out why the Nazis did it and why the German public allowed it to happen and why, when the euthanasia program was temporarily suspended in August 1941, they let the Nazis dismantle the gas chambers and take them to the concentration camps. Most importantly, I had to find out why the Nazis' attitudes toward the disabled, encapsulated in the subtle eugenics undercurrent accompanying contemporary genetics research, continued to persist. I thought I had an opportunity to show a different side of Second World War history, a side few people know about.

I completed my master's degree in 2008, and as a graduation gift my family and friends bought me a plane ticket to Germany so I could conduct research for a possible novel. In May of that year, I flew to Frankfurt and took the train northwest to Limburg. I'd booked a room at Hotel Lochmühle, and the owner's seventy-year-old mother picked me up at the train station and drove 140 kilometres an hour down the freeway. The hotel, which stood amid several hundred acres of farmland, was a forty-minute walk away from Hadamar, the small city where the Nazis' most notorious euthanasia clinic still stood. I had ten days in Germany, and my plan was to visit the clinic every day and stuff my brain with as much information as possible. No sightseeing, no festivals, no beer. I would fully employ my ability to focus, and that imaginative investment would help me recreate Germany in 1941.

Germans understand the value of history and memory. They do not attempt to erase the past; they attempt to learn from it (or at least they did then, before hate groups became popular again). When I arrived at the clinic, I recognized the building right away. It hadn't changed from the black-and-white pictures I'd seen. Even the wooden garage used to hide the buses remained.

During those ten days, I read every display, every placard, every brochure the clinic offered. I visited the burial ground behind the hospital. I met with several researchers to discuss the clinic's history. I read some of the original patient files, all of which were marked with big red plus signs to signify that euthanasia had been recommended. I filled two notebooks with questions and answers. I walked down the scuffed concrete stairwell leading to the basement. I breathed in the spongy basement scent. I noted how the concrete table in the dissection room was tilted to let blood out one end. I spent hours in the shower room, sitting in the corner and imagining what it was like for the people who were gassed and the people who did the gassing. During those ten days, something, a presence, an apparition, grey and gentle, settled onto my shoulders and never let go.

When I arrived home in Prince George, I had the entire novel in my head. I wanted to explore the personal consequences of killing large numbers of people based upon discriminatory politics and, more broadly, how what Hannah Arendt calls "the banality of evil" settles into people. I wanted to see how the euthanasia program affected those who carried out its directives, which meant choosing a Nazi as my narrator. I didn't want the usual marching, heil-Hitlering, jackboot-shining, machine-gun-toting, foaming-at-the-mouth racist. I wanted to see how a brutal ideology can slowly ruin someone young and idealistic. I wanted to see how the banality of evil seduces an intelligent person and erodes his conscience; thus, psychiatrist Michael Würfel was born.

Dr. Würfel's duty is to gas those whom the Reich has deemed a burden: namely, the disabled and the mentally ill. As the story progresses, Würfel reveals his conflicted feelings. He knows he has to take the patients down to the shower room and turn on the carbon monoxide, but he also sympathizes with the patients and questions his ability to do his duty.

I began writing the novel soon after I got home. The story came fast. The narrator, the situation, and the atmosphere were all clear to me. The grey presence I'd felt guided me as I worked; I felt totally in alignment with my material; I was writing what I was supposed to write.

My feelings were confirmed later that May when a fire gutted a Prince George plywood plant. At about

5 p.m. on the 27th, I arrived home from my government job and sat down to work on the novel. I was midway through the second chapter when I glanced out the window and saw black smoke arching across the sky. It looked exactly like the smoke I'd seen in the black-and-white photographs of Hadamar during the Second World War. It was uncanny, disconcerting, and exhilarating: what I was writing—what I was typing at that exact moment—had come to life.

The first drafts focused only on Würfel, his work in Hadamar, his transfer to the Mauthausen work camp, and finally his downfall. The novel, initially titled "Smoke," was scheduled to be published in 2012 but was later deemed gratuitously and unjustifiably violent. The publisher, who'd already signed a contract and prepared a catalogue entry for the novel, pulled the novel. Although I saw later that it was the right decision, at the time I was crushed. The novel had become an obsession, a burden. To relieve that burden, I had to share it with the world, and my publisher's decision left me exhausted and disillusioned.

I reread the manuscript a dozen times and wondered if I could tell the stories of the victims while keeping the violence, the discomfort, and Würfel's descent into evil in place. I began thinking about the buses used to transport patients from the smaller clinics to the euthanasia clinic. I began imagining a bus full of institutionalized people travelling to their deaths, with no food, no water, no bathroom breaks, and scarcely any light, because the windows were painted. I revisited my research and found a table of dates listing the number of patients put into the Hadamar gas chamber. On April 21, 1941, forty-one people with disabilities and mental illnesses were taken to the Hadamar clinic and gassed to death and burned in the crematorium. Nobody knows who they were. Maybe I could show the world some of those people.

If I were to include patients, they couldn't be pathetic Tiny Tim types. They had to be formidable, fully realized characters, people we saw and heard and felt clearly in our heads. To that end, I created seven more narrators, six of whom were patients being transferred to the clinic. As with all of my work, I wanted to show disabled people as people. I wanted to depict the inner lives of people with a variety of conditions and give each character something to which the reader could connect: a quality, an image, a desire. Judith, a young woman with Down syndrome, wants nothing more than to be clean. She believes that, if she remains clean and presentable, she will be allowed to leave the Nazis' care. She is pious and often quotes the Bible to quell her anxiety while she and her peers are being transferred. Even though other patients mock her, Judith maintains her pious nature and clean habits. Leopold has hydrocephaly, a condition that causes his skull to swell and is accompanied by epilepsy. His condition makes him extremely sensitive: every sensation grates on his nerves, and every noise shrieks along the walls of his skull. When he is not fending off the sensory assault from the people around him, he ponders his Aunt Minna's traitorous actions. Frederick is a megalomaniac and pathological liar who wants to join the Nazis not because he believes in their cause but because he believes he would make an excellent *Standartenführer*. Sebastian is a librarian accused of being a pedophile; like Frederick, he believes he is superior because of his intelligence. Nadja is an actor and comedian seized by the Nazis for resisting the Reich through her art. Her file says she has no sense of reality, but that's for the reader to decide. Emmerich, the tall young man diagnosed as feebleminded, takes the Strong but Simple Man stereotype from John Steinbeck's *Of Mice and Men* and unravels it. I wanted to show Emmerich's inner life: his relationship with his parents, his fear of his brother, and his way of perceiving the world. Emmerich is the first character to become suspicious about where the bus is going, but no one listens to him.

Waiting for the patients at the euthanasia clinic are Würfel and corpse burner Ewald. Like Würfel, Ewald faces a moral crisis: he must burn the victims' bodies while keeping his own disabled daughter a secret. He often imagines seeing his daughter among the crowd sealed into the shower room and imagines her dying frightened and alone. To fend off such thoughts, he drinks.

The story shifts from one narrator to another, building and building as the bus gets closer to the clinic, and by the time the patients arrive the reader has gotten to know them, and does not want any of them to die, and wants Würfel and Ewald to remain in alignment with their own values.

Writers who've shopped at the Store of Stereotypes leave signposts directing future writers toward the paths they've taken. These paths are so full of ruts writers think they have little choice but to resort to stereotypes. I work hard at avoiding these paths, and *The Bus* is a good example. Most novellas feature one narrator. *The Bus* has eight. I wanted to tell an exciting story while using condensed, poetic language; to achieve that, I divided the book into short chapters, each one dedicated to a different narrator. Because I prefer sparseness to inflation, I concentrated the imagery and conflict into a few pages. The result: a story wide in scope yet concentrated in effect. The novella is the angry middle child of fiction, the hungry one, the one with something to prove. It is the perfect form for writing about deafness and disability and for dissolving stereotypes in general. It is, in other words, a shopping cart built specifically for original, grain-fed, free-range products.

• • •

Eugenics is a persistent and increasingly insidious presence in our world. We often hear about fantastic new procedures that allow parents to choose what eye colour their children will have. We often read news stories about the latest advances in genetics that allow doctors to identify and pluck out genes for motley disabling conditions. When faced with the possibility of raising a child with Down syndrome or deafness, parents usually say no and abort the fetus. Ivan Carridon, my high school English teacher, once wrote a poem saying that, when it came to eugenics, Hitler wasn't a bad guy; he was just ahead of his time.

This idea that Deaf and disabled people are unwanted, in other words, has become old. Ancient even. It's also become a persistent stereotype, present in stories such as *Me Before You* and *Million Dollar Baby*.

My play *Ultrasound* is something of a sister to *The Bus*, having been fed and watered by the same source. The conflict in the play stems from a question: "In what situation would someone abort a child because it was normal?" Eugenics is the pseudo-science of suppressing or eliminating the so-called weaker members of a given population. It encourages a rigid standard of normalcy and punishes those who don't conform. I wanted to take the idea of eugenics and turn it on its head.

The situation called for someone who hated normalcy enough to give up a child; thus, Alphonse was born. I then needed a foil, someone who could coax a multitude of thoughts and emotions out of Alphonse. Why not his wife? Why not his wife who has a cochlear implant, a contentious device in the Deaf community? Why not his wife who has a cochlear implant and is comfortable with the idea of having a hearing child? Miranda, Alphonse's actor wife, came forth.

The question then became "How do I tell this story?" The idea actually started as a poem, with spoken English and American Sign Language bouncing back and forth. I thought the two languages would juxtapose in a compelling way, but it was too clumsy. The voices were too big, and the story was too complex, so I wrote it as a play.

I proceeded with total naïveté. I have no background in theatre. I'd written a few plays before, but they were horrible. I'd acted once in high school but had little to no knowledge of stagecraft, set design, blocking, lighting, or costuming. I had little to no standing in the Saskatoon Deaf community and had only a superficial knowledge of Deaf culture. I knew some Sign Language but was by no means fluent in it. I proceeded simply because I thought it was a fascinating story.

In choosing to tell a different kind of story, I had to tell the story differently, in a manner people aren't used to: that is, I had to package my grain-fed, free-range product in a custom-made, form-fitting parcel. Because I oscillate between the hearing and Deaf worlds, I wanted *Ultrasound* to be fully accessible for hearing and Deaf audience members, so I included a number of communicative elements: regular English, Shakespearean English, American Sign Language, surtitling, and heavy metal. The story is about communication and connection, and I wanted to both challenge the audience and give them an anchor to grab onto, regardless of background.

I sent the play to Yvette Nolan, who at that time—this was about February 2012—was the writer in residence at the Saskatoon Public Library. Yvette, a wonderful and gracious playwright and director, loved the play and gave me advice on how to improve it. We met several times, during which she frequently told me to "raise the stakes" in the story. She later encouraged me to submit the play to the Saskatchewan Playwrights Centre's Spring Festival, which granted *Ultrasound* a three-day workshop and a full public reading, scheduled for May 2013.

At the workshop, I discovered the extent of my naïveté and the consequences of writing something so radically different. The first day the actors, director, assistant director, interpreters, stagehands, and festival director all gathered in the rehearsal studio. There was a palpable crackle in the air as we all confronted the challenge of preparing this controversial, linguistically dense play for a public presentation. We were excited, and we were anxious. None of us was prepared. We had three days.

Unlike with the other plays at the festival, whose actors and directors no doubt focused on honing the scripts and discussing tone, motivation, and delivery, our two main tasks were to turn the script into sub-titles and to translate the English into Sign Language. At the time, I didn't know how to write a script for a signing actor; I thought that standard English would neatly translate into ASL. We ended up spending about 75 percent of our workshop on translation. Yvette, the director, was taken aback by this new challenge. She'd wanted to give the actors notes to prepare them for the reading, but the hefty translation task prevented her from doing so. When, in the midst of coming up with signs for "Shakespeare," one of the actors said that there are regional dialects of ASL and that we had to decide which regional sign to use, Yvette sighed and collapsed on the table.

"I'm sorry," I said. "I promise I'll never write anything this difficult again."

On the morning of the third day, the morning of the public reading, I arrived to find festival volunteers carrying seats into the theatre. I approached Gordon Portman, the festival director, who stood by the theatre door.

"What's going on here?" I said.

"We need the extra chairs," he said. "*Ultrasound*'s the hot show. The buzz show."

"Ah." I walked away toward our rehearsal room and added "Shit."

We spent the day preparing and reshaping the theatre, putting up a screen for the surtitles, discussing font sizes, colours, and backgrounds, and rehearsing lines. As I watched the actors, Elizabeth Morris and Peter Owusu-Ansah, I couldn't believe my audacity. How dare I write a play? What right did I have to make these poor people say and sign and toss and flick my words at the audience? The gall of me to ask that the surtitles be correct. The impudence of me to suggest a certain tone for a certain line. The nerve. The assholery. I reaffirmed my promise to Yvette: nothing this difficult ever again.

That night my wife and I arrived at the theatre to find a crowd of people streaming through the doors.

"Jesus Christ," I said.

"It'll be okay," Debbie said.

"I need a minute or two," I said.

Debbie nodded and got out of the car. I gripped the steering wheel and leaned forward, thinking I should have kept the play as a poem, or in my head, where no one could see it and no one could trudge through its tripwire density.

But then another thought arose. I remembered the first morning: the crackle, the excitement, of embarking on something entirely new. That was why people were here: to experience something radical, something completely beyond their usual experiences. I took a long breath, then got out of the car and walked inside with Debbie.

The reading was one of the most thrilling experiences of my life. More than 100 people—many of them veterans in the Saskatoon drama community—packed into the small theatre to watch Elizabeth and Peter perform. Liz and Peter did an excellent job; Liz in particular brought a rigorous vitality to the role of Miranda and maintained her high energy for more than two hours, an incredible feat considering the intense rehearsal earlier that day. The stagehand was Johnny-on-the-spot with the surtitles, which he operated from a MacBook. When the reading ended, the audience, Deaf and hearing, applauded in ASL, raising and excitedly fluttering their hands. And I saw that, despite the potential for vehement clashes, there was also the potential for dialogue, negotiation, and amity. I had to keep the play going. I had to develop it further and take it to whatever stages would welcome it.

It wasn't until three years later that *Ultrasound* was fully staged with a production that reflected the play's demands. Although there are only two characters in the play, an army of people helped put it on stage. Because the infrastructure to regularly employ Deaf theatre artists doesn't exist in Canada—meaning that interpreters and Deaf consultants who smooth out the rehearsal and production process are usually considered afterthoughts—we had to create the infrastructure. The two producing companies, Cahoots Theatre and Theatre Passe Muraille, built interpretation and consultation into their budgets from the beginning, and Theatre Passe Muraille sought an accessibility sponsor to provide ASL interpretation at the box office along with relaxed and Deaf-interpreted performances for all of the plays in its season, in addition to *Ultrasound*. The rehearsal schedule was twice as long as usual to account for the amount of time interpretation takes. In addition to the crew members—set designer, sound designer, costume designer, stage manager, and their assistants—we had a projection artist and a surtitle operator, not to mention a bevy of interpreters who ensured steady communication between the director, Marjorie Chan, and the actors (while Liz Morris remained in the role of Miranda, Chris Dodd was chosen to play Alphonse). Cahoots also budgeted enough money to create the Deaf Artists and Theatres Toolkit (DATT), a free online resource for theatres interested in working with Deaf artists and audience members. The DATT addresses virtually every aspect of theatre production, from budgeting and box office relations to marketing and performance interpretation.

Ultrasound opened on the main stage at Theatre Passe Muraille on May 2, 2016. Both Debbie and my mom attended with me. Although I'd seen the play's previews, I still had difficulty keeping my supper down that night.

The play represented a significant shift in Canadian theatre. Not only did it feature two Deaf actors in roles created by a deaf playwright on one of the most venerated stages in Canada, but also it showed audiences the artistic and logistical possibilities. It showed them the potential of telling stories from a Deaf perspective.

It showed them what a fully accessible play looked like and challenged theatres across the country to make their plays more accessible.

ON IDEAS

When an idea arises, I let it gestate for months, often years. I never start writing about it immediately. If over time the characters make me laugh or drag a cold claw over my heart, and if the situation is bizarre and continues to snag my attention, then eventually I write the story.

Ideas typically come in two forms: as a voice or as a situation. *Mantis Dreams* began with a voice yammering in my head. I was struck by its force, the way it plowed forward with a conviction I'd never experienced. It was propulsive, rowdy, caustic, and insightful, often at the same time. As time passed, it grew stronger and louder; it began to form a personality. Many thoughts criticized academics and scholarly institutions, pointing out their hypocrisy and inflated self-importance. I tried to ignore these thoughts, because they were distracting me from my PhD work, but after four or five months they built up too much momentum to ignore, and I had to write them down. I thought writing them down would silence them, silence that voice, but it kept speaking. I set aside my dissertation work to write down these strange, hilarious, and heartbreaking thoughts. The voice made me laugh every time I sat down to write. It—he—said things I never could. He surprised me. He showed me how ridiculous and brilliant and aggravating human beings can be. Within a few months, I had the first draft of a book, and a year and a half later it became my first published novel.

I'm pretty sure my speech therapy has something to do with the voices that rattle in my head. Because I've spent so much time pretending to be Ace Ventura and Jim Hughson and Krusty the Clown and Invader Zim and Saul Goodman and countless other people, it's become natural for me first to give voice to my own characters and then to follow their voices into whatever situations arise.

When I was twenty or so, I watched a made-for-TV film called *The Brooke Ellison Story*. Directed by Christopher Reeve, the film focused on a woman named Brooke Ellison, who became a quadriplegic after a car accident. She overcame a number of obstacles and eventually graduated from Harvard University. The film was a maudlin mess and made Brooke's journey much too easy. It did, however, trigger a question in my brain. How did she express herself sexually?

The question persisted in my mind, and three or four months later I started writing a short story called "The Crooked Tree." In it a teenage girl named Jacqueline struggles with her sexual maturity; living in a small town (Ashcroft) and being a quadriplegic make things even more challenging. She's attracted to her friend Connor but constantly bothered by a young man with an intellectual disability named Desmond. Desmond wants to be Jacqueline's boyfriend; in his mind, disabled people should date other disabled people. Jacqueline resists, though, and at one point Desmond attempts to win her affections by giving her food. She presses her lips together. Desmond pushes the spoon against her mouth, spilling the food. "Fuck off!" Jacqueline cries, everyone in the cafeteria turning to look at them. The story ends with Jacqueline inviting Connor to their favourite spot, an isolated and shady area underneath a twisted apricot tree. Connor has to leave for the summer to work for his father, and her urge to express herself sexually, to experience pleasure even if it's through giving pleasure, takes over. She asks Connor to put his penis into her mouth. Connor refuses. Jacqueline asks him again. After a tense negotiation and a few tears, Connor relents. Just as he puts his penis into her mouth, they hear a sound in the bushes and see Desmond running back into town to tell Jacqueline's mother. The story was forty pages long, much too long, I thought, for a literary journal, until *Pages of Stories* bought it in April 2010.

I find that ideas based upon situation don't have the same urgency as ideas based upon voice. A clear voice that hooks you by the eyes and tears across the page is one of the best—if not the best—pleasures of reading. The voice looks to make trouble, and you simply follow it; the situation is just there, and it's up to you to use it to make trouble.

During Christmas of 2016, my wife and I were sitting in the living room watching *Emmet Otter's Jug-Band Christmas*. It was evening. We'd plugged the tree in, and at one point I turned to look at it. I noticed Debbie looking at me—studying me with those beautiful dappled blue eyes of hers.

"Why are you looking at me like that?" I said.

"Your eyes," she said. "They're so loving and full of awe and wonder."

"They're full of awe and wonder," I said, "because I never understand what the fuck's going on."

Debbie laughed. So did I.

Because of my deafness, I often don't fully understand what goes on around me. As a result, I'm endlessly curious. If I find an idea that's worthwhile, I don't stop clawing back layers until I reach the slimy, seizing, jagged tumour, the shit-smeared kernel that reveals everything the reader needs to know about a character and the world in which she lives.

Discovery has a price, though. From the time I wrote the first draft to the book's publication, *The Bus* took eight years to share with the world. In those eight years, I lived in that headspace, that basement place swollen with the scents of burning human flesh and sweat and shit and piss and blood and confusion and anger and helplessness. My heart darkened—I thought the worst about people. I thought human beings had a bottom-less capacity for cruelty, especially toward those they considered different. I thought human beings were fools who could not distinguish between good and evil. I thought their creativity showed up best when they came up with ways to kill one another. I couldn't protect myself, though. There is no prophylactic for curiosity. To write this story truthfully, I had to follow my curiosity up humanity's polyp-ridden asshole and confront its worst qualities.

The price was worth it. I'm proud of *The Bus*, and I like to think I'm a bit wiser for having written it.

ON TEXT

My defence for my master's degree was a nightmare.

It was in April 2008. The previous weekend my volleyball team had won a tournament in Fort St. James, BC, fuelling my confidence. I knew my material backward, forward, and upside down. I had an excellent relationship with my supervisor, who'd helped me smooth out the rougher parts of my thesis.

Still, my defence was a nightmare.

My external examiner was unable to come to Prince George from her home in Windsor. We tried to set up Skype so I could read her lips, but it didn't work, so we had to set up a conference-style telephone in the classroom where my defence was held, allowing the examiner to relay her questions through a set of tinny speakers.

I dressed up in a suit and tie. Some of my friends and fellow students had come, as did my mom, who'd driven up to PG from Kamloops. I'd prepared and rehearsed a PowerPoint presentation summarizing the key arguments of my thesis.

A typical defence begins with the candidate presenting their work before being questioned by the examiners. At my defence, I walked in and sat down. My first slide, which showed the title of my thesis, was projected on a screen behind me.

The chair of my defence sat down and stacked some pages in front of him. "Okay, hello, everyone. And welcome. Today we have Mr. Adam Pottle, who is defending his thesis in order to receive his master's degree. So the way it works is that the four examiners, the three in the room here and our external, on the phone, will ask their questions, to which Adam will respond. Once Adam has responded to their questions, we can open things up to the rest of the crowd, in case anyone else has anything they'd like to know. I believe we'll begin with the external examiner."

I started to raise my hand. "Wait a—"

A squelch of static. A hollow rattle. "Okay. Ah-dam?"

"Yes."

"Canoo hew meh?"

The examiner's words sounded as though they were spoken through a brass pipe.

"I think so."

"Greay. Wensafdel inos mellibluddelteffering questionszink sospaoosability teppeddityvolk-ernegklin your vixxerklees quessipeddolongo,

cibbalantickorckerwenneth. You mahnshunmfurg-
burgburg curring vyuen roign calksstiffepewlesszerop.
Dobeddbanlasdack tupoednasoidroidpled mehntmahn
asforstbunckwhengleen, but artenlubbel offerlingpertch-
newzecxmiln whiqueftbub calsloch amslip furten, xim-
mumurmumber plotzchenkenliber optwentlinkleslee?"

I stared forward. I met eyes with my mom. She
understood immediately.

"I'm sorry, what did you say, Professor?"

"Horkenflerken onlenjurkenbadt soleenehdt twinnd-
unck werdtenden queetliekbollptirt. Ertay?"

"Did you hear, Adam?" the chair said.

"No."

Consulting with the examiner, the chair did his
best to repeat her question. I blushed. My brain, which
ten minutes earlier had been tightly wound and laser-
focused, slackened, collapsed, ideas and words splat-
tering all over the bottom of my skull. My breathing
quickened. I looked at my supervisor, pleading, accus-
ing. Why hadn't I been asked to present my research?
Why couldn't someone type the examiner's words? Why
couldn't the examiner submit her questions on paper or
through other means?

My in-person examiners asked three or four questions each. I could understand them, but I eked out my
answers. I was rattled from not being able to hear the
external examiner.

By the time I was asked to leave the room so the
examiners could deliberate, I'd almost imploded into a
pile of pulsing nerves. I stepped outside and loosened
my tie and cranked my head to the ceiling and concentrated on straightening my breathing. Mom and my
friends joined me.

"You did good, hon," Mom said.

"That was a fucking joke," I said. "I couldn't understand a damn thing she was saying."

"I know. You still did well."

"How can they tell? How do you evaluate that? Shit." I hunched over. "If I don't pass—"

"You'll be fine. You answered the ones where they were in the room."

Fifteen minutes later—much later than I'd have liked—I was called back in.

"Congratulations!" the external examiner said. The one relevant word I heard.

I passed, though I had some minor revisions to make before my thesis would be acceptable enough for me to graduate. Despite the hugs and handshakes, I left my defence feeling unworthy, as though I'd compromised my values. The central idea of my thesis was that deafness and disability constitute personal identities rather than social stigmas, that a deaf or disabled person should feel proud rather than ashamed, yet we couldn't find an accessible way for me to receive my examiner's questions.

Eight years later, on February 26, 2016, I defended my PhD dissertation. Again I'd written about deafness and disability. Again I knew the material every which way. Again I had an excellent relationship with my supervisors. There were two key differences, though: my external examiner, Karen Yoshida, flew in from Toronto, and the English department, at my request, hired a real-time captioning typist to ensure I understood every question.

We all gathered in a small classroom on the tenth floor of the University of Saskatchewan arts building— my five examiners, the graduate chair, my friends, my fellow grad students, the typist, and my wife. After I

presented my research—and took my sweet time in
doing so—the chair asked Professor Yoshida to present
her questions. She leaned forward and smiled.

With real-time captioning, a typist uses a short-
hand keyboard to keep up with the conversation, the
words appearing on a computer or projection screen.
The following question and response are taken from
the typist's transcription, which the typist sent to me a
month after my defence. I've edited a few small things
for clarity.

> First of all, Adam, I wanted to say what
> a delight it was to read your thesis, and
> it was a real pleasure. I didn't see it as
> work, actually. I thought it was a pleasure
> reading. You have done such a marvellous
> job, and you and your committee and all
> your readership should be congratulated
> for all your efforts and work. I want to
> start off with a methodological question,
> if I could. You were very clear with what
> the criteria was for novels to be chosen
> for your thesis, so I wanted to know what
> the process was to decide to analyze these
> particular seven ones, seven novels.

I took my time reading Professor Yoshida's words.
When I was ready, I put my hands together.

> I chose these seven novels because they,
> to me, they presented some of the most
> dynamic portrayals of disability in Ca-
> nadian literature. As I mentioned in my
> presentation, it's very rare to find a novel

in Canadian literature that focuses on a main character with a disability. And I can name a number of other novels that have characters with disabilities, but the thing is disability doesn't form the core of the narrative, where the disabled character . . . is not the main character. So the reason I chose those seven novels specifically is because they had that main character in place.

Each question came clearly, and I responded with equally clear answers. Five examiners questioned me, and I answered each question immediately. I not only wanted my doctorate but also wanted to rinse out the bitterness left by my master's defence and, by using captioning, assert my dissertation's central theme of inclusivity by showing an example of a more open and accessible world.

An hour and a half later, when I was sent out of the room so the examiners could deliberate, I had no doubt.

When they called me back seven minutes later, my supervisor said, "Congratulations, Dr. Pottle." I shook hands with each of my examiners.

The graduate chair said, "People were very, very positive about your oral defence. They said you did a stellar job."

To which I responded, "As a deaf man, you can't imagine what that means to me."

Had I not had the captioning, I doubt I would have done so well on my defence. Text has a soothing effect on me, and I've come to realize how my deafness has given me an intimate relationship with text. I'm most comfortable with text: text in a book, text on my phone, text on closed captioning, text on the screens at the grocery store, text on the specials board at a restaurant. Text is my safe zone, my blanket, my lens, the thing that anchors me to and allows me to access reality. Things don't become real for me unless I read them. If an elevator's out of order, or if a highway's blocked off, or if a building's being evacuated, I need textual confirmation; otherwise, I don't believe it.

In *Beautiful Mutants*, I talk about a city made of language. In my ideal world, every sound is textually expressed. When people speak, words drift out of their mouths, and their words have colours and fonts that suit their personalities: the words of a bubbly man might be bright green **Broadway**, whereas the words of a melancholy woman might be dark red Centaur. Birdsong floats in dazzling yellow notes; thunder stomps through the sky in black-and-blue blocks; a German shepherd's bark shoots from its mouth like brown thorns; screeching tires leave white scratch marks on the air. In my ideal world, everyone's story is written on the air for me to read.

I'm incredibly picky about fonts. I'd make great friends with a typesetter. My pickiness stems from the way I experience language: words have a sensual feeling for me, so I need fonts that don't prick my finger or jam my sinuses. If I'm at the bookstore and I see a book printed in a font that doesn't appeal to me, I won't buy the book. Doesn't matter if it's the next *Harry Potter* or *Fear and Loathing in Las Vegas*. Fonts affect the way I experience stories and poems, which means they must cohere with their contents. A grim story told in an open, inviting font such as **Bookman Old Style** jars against my eyes, and a bizarre, twisted story told in a flat font such as **Arial** galls and frustrates me.

Garamond is my go-to font for writing. I use it in everything I do. It's the Michael Fassbender of fonts: it can handle a range of subjects, from historical adventure to tragicomedy. I also appreciate its efficiency; it doesn't take any more space than it has to, and as a writer who values sparseness I respect that.

Captioning has had not only an aesthetic influence in terms of shaping my font choices and my poetic lines and my fictional dialogue but also an ontological influence. Years of watching captioned shows have created a reliance on text while demonstrating how to use text to drive a story and stimulate the thoughts and emotions of others. By listening to, watching, and reading TV shows and films—by hearing and reading countless gasps, sighs, explosions, shootings, stabbings, fuckings, rustles, scrapes, punches, and taps—I've learned how to make text thick with sound.

One of my favourite horror films is *Halloween*. I first saw it when I was five years old, and have seen it dozens of times over the years, but until recently it was impossible to find a captioned version. It mattered little, though. Horror relies more on image and silence to tell the story than most other film genres, so it was easy for me to piece the story together by just watching the actors. If I ever wondered what Dr. Loomis was saying to Sheriff Brackett, or what Laurie was saying to Annie, I asked my dad or brother.

Twenty-six years later I finally found a *Halloween* DVD with captioning. Watching the film with captioning added another layer to it. The dialogue deepened the subtexts—the psychological background, the male-female conflict—but most interesting were the sound effects, particularly Michael Myers's breathing when the camera showed his point of view. I'd never

heard Michael breathing before, yet there were the captions saying "[HEAVY BREATHING]." Before, Michael had
been a ghoul-like figure, but knowing he was breathing
somehow seemed to humanize him. He was evil yet
of this world. It made the character more real to me;
also, his breathing was heavy, implying heat and even
discomfort behind his mask. It lent an additional layer
to the film's male-female dynamic, suggesting he was
the perverted Everyman.

The most impactful captions arise at the end of the
film. After Loomis shoots Michael six times, sending
him off a balcony into the front yard, Laurie utters her
famous line "It *was* the bogeyman," to which Loomis
responds "As a matter of fact, it was." Loomis then
walks to the balcony and finds that Michael's body is
gone. The film ends with a series of shots showing all of
the places where Michael was: the stairwell, the living
room, the exterior of the Wallace house, the abandoned
Myers house.

Before I watched the film with captions, I never
fully understood why John Carpenter showed all those
places, but as I watched it with captions I saw again the
"[HEAVY BREATHING]," and a fresh fear arose, the kind
of fear I experienced when I first saw the film as a kid.
Michael could be anywhere.

It's not just the captioning that has influenced me
but also how the words interact with sound and image.
In *The Bus*, Leopold, the young man with hydrocephaly,
thinks his fellow patients' voices "sound like dumping
gravel in a puddle." When I first wrote that line, I both
saw it and heard it. It appeared as an image and a sound
and as words. I experienced the sound in three sensual
planes, all of which I attempted to distill into text. Later
in the story, the librarian Sebastian sees one of his fellow

patients get shot by a guard: "His machine gun jars and fires, a quick, fierce clatter." Gunshots are over quickly, hence one-word descriptions like *bang, boom, crash*. I wanted to slow down Sebastian's words by describing the gunshots in detail. Sebastian has affection for the patient who is shot, so the impact is somewhat in slow motion for him. I began with *quick* because obviously machine guns shoot quickly, but then I added a comma, followed by another adjective, *fierce*. I love this word: when you say it, you end up looking like you've bitten down on something. I used the word *clatter* because I wanted to capture the normalization of the sound in war. Many other things clatter. Dishes clatter. Vehicles clatter. Containers and boxes and drawers clatter. As with Leopold's description, these words arose as image, sound, and word.

Smells and touches operate the same way. When Ewald, the corpse burner, inhales "the hot, filthy odour from the oven," I smell it, see it, and read it. Near the end of the journey by bus, pathological liar Frederick observes that "Everyone's sickness browns the air." Every sense has a visual component to accompany the captioning aspect. A reddish-black trail drifts from the oven and hooks its fingers into Ewald's nose (and my nose); the patients' blood and vomit and shit and piss curdle into a nauseating scent that colours the air a splotchy beige. Within my head operates a unique synesthesia, resulting in a textual synthesis that's evolved from years of observing the world from a deaf perspective.

• • •

Embedded in my relationship with text is a simple yet elemental fact: I write because it's what I'm built to do.

I wouldn't be a writer if I wasn't deaf. Everything—my imagination, my capacity to observe, my voice, my relationship with text, my comfort with silence and solitude—has grown out of my deafness. My deafness has made me into a writer, and writing has become my way of fully inhabiting the world.

WHAT KIND OF DEAF MAN? (A BRIEF REPRISE)

n July 2017, shortly after my appointment with the otolaryngologist, I was invited to read at the Word on the Street Festival in Saskatoon in September. I'd read at the festival twice before, and I accepted the invitation with gratitude.

My last appearance had been three years earlier. I read with two other writers, and I couldn't understand what they were reading despite sitting beside them. This time I wanted to absorb all of their words, as well as understand the audience's questions, so I asked for real-time captioning and ASL interpretation. Because I knew that accessibility supports can be costly, I offered to waive my author's fee to pay for them; the festival organizer said she'd need to speak to the board.

A month later, on August 25, the organizer responded. The festival couldn't provide the supports I'd requested.

I emailed her back: "Did you tell the board I'm willing to waive my reading fee? And does this news mean I'm no longer being asked to read? If I am still being asked to read, I can try and arrange accessibility measures myself, if that's okay."

She responded quickly: "After the board discussion I presumed we were going to have to proceed without your involvement, and the program has been finalized now. I'm sorry it's not going to work out for this year."

Not only was I not going to receive captioning and ASL interpretation, but also I was being dropped from the festival completely.

The news hurt. As with most Deaf and disabled artists—hell, as with most artists, period—I seldom have the opportunity to present my work in such a prominent public setting, and to be ousted because I requested accessibility supports was painful, not to mention discriminatory.

At the time I received the news, my wife and I were on our way home from a family reunion in BC. As we drove through Edmonton, I checked my Twitter account and noticed a discussion about accessibility and literary events. Several disabled artists bemoaned the lack of accessible facilities that prevented them from attending events and supporting authors. I joined in the conversation and mentioned what had happened to me. I put my phone away and chatted with my wife for a few hours.

At our next stop, in North Battleford, I checked Twitter again. My page had blown up—by my standards, anyway, since I had only a few hundred followers at the time. Disability artists, advocates, and allies from across North America had followed me and tweeted at me and at the festival, supporting my right to accessibility

supports and demanding that I be reinstated, with captioning and ASL interpretation.

The furor increased over the next two days. Advocates emailed the festival and tweeted at other festival
authors, asking them if they supported the festival's
actions. The festival emailed me; its organizers hadn't
expected such a response. Abled people seldom expect
Deaf and disabled people to protest, believing they are
either incapable of making a difference or too small a
community to do so. There are over one billion Deaf and
disabled people in the world, with over four million in
Canada. It's a potent chorus.

After several emails from different festival board
members, the president of the festival board emailed
me on August 28:

> Although not as we would have hoped,
> but nonetheless sincerely and enthusias-
> tically extended, we officially extend an
> invitation to you to be on the roster of
> presenting authors on September 24th.
> The details of presentation will need to
> be sorted out, as well as the technical
> details of your supporting aids, but our
> Board is committed to ensuring you are
> well supported, and that those within the
> deaf and hearing impaired community
> have accessibility to your program. Addi-
> tionally, this situation has ... [prompted]
> our Board to consider future planning
> and budgetary needs for accessibility, not
> previously requested.

I thanked the president and tweeted the news and expressed my gratitude to the festival for being willing to learn and to my fellow artists, advocates, and allies for their support.

On September 24, I proudly stood at the podium and read from *The Bus*, and when I was finished I took questions, all of which were clearly typed on the captioning screen and interpreted for Deaf audience members, and at the end I thanked the captionist, the interpreter, the festival, and the audience, and I asked the audience to applaud in Sign Language, raising their hands and fluttering them in the air. I snapped a picture of it and tweeted "This is what better looks like."

• • •

Even after all this, though, I'm still not sure what kind of deaf man I want to be. I think it's impossible to know because my deafness evolves, and so do I. Categories are useful to everyone who exists outside them. I adapt with hearing aids and Sign Language and captioning and texting.

I never got the cochlear implant. I don't think I ever will. The idea of someone drilling a hole into my head and inserting an electronic apparatus is a bit too *Matrix*-like for me. I'm paranoid that someone will invent a computer program that turns cochlear implants into mind-control devices.

I did get a hearing aid, though. On Valentine's Day 2018, I was fitted with a two-thousand-dollar, behind-the-ear, skin-coloured Phonak unit. What better way to celebrate love than to hear your wife's voice distorted by squelching static?

Although birds and whistles are more annoying than I thought they'd be, I've gotten used to the hearing aid. It's easier than when I was a kid, partly because the technology's improved and partly because I need it more now.

Just as my deafness evolves, so too does the way I write. I started writing when I was sixteen, but I didn't become a writer until I started exploring deafness and disability. To write, to create in our information-soaked world, is to exist in a perpetual state of becoming. Writing about these subjects required me to overcome my own discomfort—I couldn't do it until I was ready. Since then, I've been writing my way into deafness, burrowing into it like a tarantula, gradually becoming more and more comfortable with it, though never completely comfortable. My deafness is neither a gift nor a curse. It's a genetic anomaly that governs the way I perceive the world and, in doing so, influences the direction of my life. On some days, I'm grateful for my deafness, and on others I resent it. But I'll always be deaf, hearing aid or no hearing aid, implant or no implant. And I'll always write.

ACKNOWLEDGEMENTS

Bruce Walsh for inviting me to write this book and provoking me into thinking about these things.

Karen Clark and the staff at University of Regina Press for getting behind this book from the start.

Jeanette Lynes for her compassionate and steady editorial hand.

Bruce Hunter for his guidance, encouragement, and companionship.

Brad Fraser, whose saying "If it doesn't scare you, it's not worth writing" prodded me as I wrote.

Vici Johnstone and her staff at Caitlin Press for giving me a chance and printing *Beautiful Mutants* and *Mantis Dreams*.

Luciano Iacobelli, Sonia D'Agostino, and everyone at Quattro Books for selecting *The Bus* as the Ken Klonsky winner and publishing the book after an eight-year effort.

All those who have supported my writing and my efforts to make literary events more accessible, namely Dorothy Ellen Palmer, Jael Richardson, Jane Eaton Hamilton, and Amanda Leduc.

Auntie Jeannie and Uncle Dan for helping me remember Kitimat details—especially the bike story.

Mom, Dad, and Taylor for the memories and endless support.

Debbie. Always.

SELECTED REFERENCES AND CREDITS

Writers / Books Quoted or Discussed

Hannah Arendt, *Eichmann in Jerusalem: A Report on the Banality of Evil.*

Kim Clark, *A One-Handed Novel.*

William Faulkner, *As I Lay Dying.*

Brad Fraser, *Kill Me Now, Unidentified Human Remains and the True Nature of Love.*

David Freeman, *Creeps.*

Jane Eaton Hamilton, *Weekend.*

Tomson Highway, *Kiss of the Fur Queen.*

Bruce Hunter, *Two O'Clock Creek: Poems New and Selected.*

Ilya Kaminsky, *Dancing in Odessa, Deaf Republic.*

Stephen King, *On Writing: A Memoir of the Craft.*

Ryan Knighton, *Cockeyed.*

Ann-Marie MacDonald, *Fall on Your Knees.*

Cormac McCarthy, *No Country for Old Men, The Road.*

Toni Morrison, *Beloved, Sula.*

Dorothy Ellen Palmer, *When Fenelon Falls.*

Leah Lakshmi Piepzna-Samarasinha, *Bodymap.*

Adam Pottle, *Beautiful Mutants, The Bus, Mantis Dreams: The Journal of Dr. Dexter Ripley, Ultrasound.*

Mordecai Richler, *The Apprenticeship of Duddy Kravitz, Barney's Version.*

Eden Robinson, *Monkey Beach, Son of a Trickster.*

Hunter S. Thompson, *Fear and Loathing in Las Vegas.*

Richard Van Camp, *Angel Wing Splash Pattern, The Lesser Blessed.*

Elie Wiesel, *Night.*

Tom Wolfe, *The Electric Kool-Aid Acid Test.*

Articles / Interviews / Poems / Speeches

Austin Chisholm, "In Darkness, Ryan Knighton Found His Voice," interview with Ryan Knighton, *The Tyee*, June 5, 2015, https://thetyee.ca/Culture/2015/06/05/Ryan-Knighton-Author/.

Jennifer James, "The *Split This Rock* Interview with Ilya Kaminsky," *Split This Rock*, April 9, 2018, http://blogthisrock.blogspot.com/2018/04/the-split-this-rock-interview-with-ilya.html.

Ilya Kaminsky, "From *Deaf Republic*: 2. 9AM Bombardment," *Poetry Foundation*, May 2009, https://www.poetryfoundation.org/poetrymagazine/poems/52520/deaf-republic-2-9am-bombardment.

Jen Sookfong Lee, "On Respectable Narratives and Why Diversity Matters on the Page," *Open Book*, April 25, 2018, http://open-book.ca/Columnists/On-respectable-narratives-and-why-diversity-on-the-page-matters.

Elie Wiesel, "The Nobel Peace Prize Acceptance Speech Delivered by Elie Wiesel in Oslo on December 10, 1986," in *Night* (New York: Hill and Wang, 2006).

Excerpt Credits

Bruce Hunter excerpt from "The Scale" in *Two O'Clock Creek: Poems New and Selected*. Copyright (c) 2010. Reprinted with permission of Oolichan Books.

Ilya Kaminsky excerpt from "9AM Bombardment" from Deaf Republic. Originally published in *Poetry* (May 2009). Copyright (c) 2009, 2018 by Ilya Kaminsky. Reprinted with the permission of The PermissionsCompany, Inc., on behalf of Graywolf Press, Minneapolis, Minnesota, www.graywolfpress.org.

Adam Pottle excerpts from *Beautiful Mutants* (2011) and *Mantis Dreams* (2013) reprinted with permission of Caitlin Press.

ABOUT THE AUTHOR

Adam Pottle's writing explores the dynamic and philosophical aspects of Deafness and disability. Adam has
a PhD in English literature and is the author of a play,
Ultrasound, a volume of poetry, *Beautiful Mutants*, a
novel, *Mantis Dreams: The Journal of Dr. Dexter Ripley*,
and a novella, *The Bus*. He lives in Saskatoon.